PINHOK™
LANGUAGES

www.pinhok.com

Introduction

This Book

This vocabulary guide contains all 5000 HSK vocabularies grouped by level starting from HSK 1 and finishing with HSK 6. The vocabularies are based on the changes from 2012 and all come with Pinyin and English translation. If you are just starting out preparing for an HSK test, this book is ideal to slowly and step by step build the vocabulary you need to successfully pass whatever level it is you are aiming for. Shortly before the test, the book can again be very helpful in acting as a checklist to see which words haven't been learned yet or need to be studied again.

As common with most vocabulary books, it's possible to study from Chinese to English as well as English to Chinese. Chinese to English provides you with the opportunity to make quick progress in areas like listening and reading. English to Chinese on the other hand allows you to practice your writing and also has positive effects on your speaking skills. To successfully pass any of the 6 HSK levels there are further topics for you to consider like grammar or listening which are not covered in this book. This book concentrates on helping you to build the foundation that allows you to then accelerate further learning in courses, with mock exams or whatever other form of studying works best for you. Good luck!

Pinhok Languages

Pinhok Languages strives to create language learning products that support learners around the world in their mission of learning a new language. In doing so, we combine best practice from various fields and industries to come up with innovative products and material.

The Pinhok Team hopes this book can help you with your learning process and gets you to your goal faster. Should you be interested in finding out more about us, please go to our website www.pinhok.com. For feedback, error reports, criticism or simply a quick "hi", please also go to our website and use the contact form.

Disclaimer of Liability

HSK 1

我	wǒ	Pronoun: I
你	nǐ	Pronoun: you (singular)
我们	wǒ men	Pronoun: we
他	tā	Pronoun: he
她	tā	Pronoun: she
爱	ài	Verb: to love
喜欢	xǐ huan	Verb: to like
很	hěn	Adverb: very, quite
都	dōu	Adverb: all, both Pronoun: all, both
和	hé	Relative Clause: with Conjunction: and
高兴	gāo xìng	Adjective: happy, glad, cheerful
漂亮	piào liang	Adjective: pretty, beautiful
个	gè	Measure Word: for almost everything
这	zhè	Pronoun: this
那	nà	Pronoun: that
些	xiē	Measure Word: some, few, several
是	shì	Verb: is, to be
的	de	Particle: to form an attribute
朋友	péng you	Noun: friend
好	hǎo	Adjective: good, nice
人	rén	Noun: person, people
了	le	Particle: indicating past or change
太	tài	Adverb: too, extremely
衣服	yī fu	Noun: clothes
买	mǎi	Verb: to buy
大	dà	Adjective: big, great

小	xiǎo	Adjective: small
不	bù	Adverb: no, not
有	yǒu	Verb: to have, to exist, to be
没有	méi yǒu	Verb: to not have
钱	qián	Noun: money
吗	ma	Particle: to form a question
呢	ne	Particle: to build a question based on already mentioned subjects
谁	shéi	Pronoun: who
什么	shén me	Pronoun: what
书	shū	Noun: book
本	běn	Noun: root, basis, foundation, origin, capital Measure Word: for books, files, etc.
哪	nǎ	Pronoun: which
几	jǐ	Adverb: how many Pronoun: several
多少	duō shao	Adverb: how many, how much
多	duō	Adjective: much, many
少	shǎo	Adjective: few, little
怎么	zěn me	Adverb: how
怎么样	zěn me yàng	Adverb: how is/are Expression: how about that?
天气	tiān qì	Noun: weather
里	lǐ	Location: in, inside Measure Word: for 0.5km
在	zài	Relative Clause: at, on, in Particle: for action in progress
哪儿	nǎr	Pronoun: where
冷	lěng	Adjective: cold
热	rè	Adjective: hot, warm
住	zhù	Verb: to live, to stay, to reside
北京	Běi jīng	Noun: Beijing
中国	Zhōng guó	Noun: China

去	qù	Verb: to go
来	lái	Verb: to come, to arrive Particle: ever since
上	shàng	Verb: to go up, to attend, to climb Location: on, upon, previous, upper
下	xià	Verb: descend, fall Measure Word: for times of action Location: below, down, under
工作	gōng zuò	Noun: job Verb: to work
医生	yī shēng	Noun: doctor
医院	yī yuàn	Noun: hospital
商店	shāng diàn	Noun: shop, store
前面	qián miàn	Location: ahead, in front
后面	hòu miàn	Location: rear, back, behind
先生	xiān sheng	Noun: Mister (Mr.), teacher
十	shí	Number: 10
一	yī	Number: 1
二	èr	Number: 2
三	sān	Number: 3
四	sì	Number: 4
五	wǔ	Number: 5
六	liù	Number: 6
七	qī	Number: 7
八	bā	Number: 8
九	jiǔ	Number: 9
点	diǎn	Noun: point, dot Verb: to nod, to click Measure Word: a little, a bit
一点儿	yī diǎnr	Adverb: a bit, a little
现在	xiàn zài	Time: now
分钟	fēn zhōng	Noun: minute
上午	shàng wǔ	Noun: morning

中午	zhōng wǔ	Noun: noon, midday
下午	xià wǔ	Noun: afternoon
时候	shí hou	Noun: time, moment, period
昨天	zuó tiān	Time: yesterday
今天	jīn tiān	Time: today
明天	míng tiān	Time: tomorrow
月	yuè	Noun: month, moon
说	shuō	Verb: to say, to speak
年	nián	Noun: year
星期	xīng qī	Noun: week
东西	dōng xi	Noun: thing
吃	chī	Verb: to eat
喝	hē	Verb: to drink
茶	chá	Noun: tea
小姐	xiǎo jiě	Noun: Miss, young lady
菜	cài	Noun: dish, vegetable
米饭	mǐ fàn	Noun: (cooked) rice
块	kuài	Measure Word: for a piece
杯子	bēi zi	Noun: cup, glass
请	qǐng	Verb: to ask, to invite Expression: please
坐	zuò	Verb: to sit, to take (bus, train, etc.)
椅子	yǐ zi	Noun: chair
桌子	zhuō zi	Noun: table
狗	gǒu	Noun: dog
猫	māo	Noun: cat
谢谢	xiè xie	Expression: thanks!
不客气	bú kè qi	Expression: you are welcome
做	zuò	Verb: to do, to make

会	huì	Noun: meeting, conference Auxiliary Verb: can, to be able to
能	néng	Auxiliary Verb: to be able to
水	shuǐ	Noun: water
开	kāi	Verb: to open, to start, to drive (car, etc.)
水果	shuǐ guǒ	Noun: fruit
苹果	píng guǒ	Noun: apple
叫	jiào	Verb: to be called, to call, to shout
名字	míng zi	Noun: name
岁	suì	Measure Word: "years old"
妈妈	mā ma	Noun: mum
爸爸	bà ba	Noun: dad
儿子	ér zi	Noun: son
女儿	nǚ ér	Noun: daughter
家	jiā	Noun: family, home, household Measure Word: for businesses, families
想	xiǎng	Verb: to think, to miss Auxiliary Verb: to want
回	huí	Verb: to return, to answer, to reply Measure Word: for events of action
看见	kàn jiàn	Verb: to see, to catch sight of
饭店	fàn diàn	Noun: restaurant
飞机	fēi jī	Noun: airplane
出租车	chū zū chē	Noun: taxi
再见	zài jiàn	Expression: goodbye, see you
看	kàn	Verb: to see, to watch, to look at
电影	diàn yǐng	Noun: movie, film
电视	diàn shì	Noun: TV(-set)
电脑	diàn nǎo	Noun: computer
睡觉	shuì jiào	Verb: to sleep, to go to bed
打电话	dǎ diàn huà	Verb: to make a phone call

喂	wéi	Expression: hello (phone)
下雨	xià yǔ	Verb: to rain
对不起	duì bu qǐ	Expression: sorry, I'm sorry
认识	rèn shi	Noun: understanding, knowledge, awareness Verb: to know, to recognize, to understand, to be familiar with
没关系	méi guān xi	Expression: it doesn't matter
学校	xué xiào	Noun: school
读	dú	Verb: to read
学习	xué xí	Verb: to study, to learn
汉语	hàn yǔ	Noun: Chinese language
学生	xué sheng	Noun: student, pupil
同学	tóng xué	Noun: classmate
老师	lǎo shī	Noun: teacher
听	tīng	Verb: to listen, to hear, to obey Measure Word: for canned beverages
号	hào	Noun: number, day of month
字	zì	Noun: word, character
写	xiě	Verb: to write

往	wǎng	Verb: to go Relative Clause: towards, to
男	nán	Adjective: male
虽然 x 但是 y	suī rán x dàn shì y	Conjunction: although x, y
女	nǚ	Adjective: female
因为 x 所以 y	yīn wèi x suǒ yǐ y	Conjunction: because of x, y
一下	yī xià	Expression: to suggest to give it a go Number: once
对	duì	Relative Clause: for, to, towards
非常	fēi cháng	Adverb: very
最	zuì	Adverb: most
比	bǐ	Relative Clause: than, used for comparison
得	de	Particle: used to link verb with adjective
您	nín	Pronoun: you (singular, polite)
它	tā	Pronoun: it
大家	dà jiā	Pronoun: everybody, all
一起	yì qǐ	Adverb: together
为什么	wèi shén me	Adverb: why
吧	ba	Particle: indicating suggestion
过	guo	Particle: indicating action in the past
着	zhe	Particle: indicating action in progress
要	yào	Auxiliary Verb: to want to, going to
正在	zhèng zài	Adverb: in the process of, in course of
已经	yǐ jīng	Adverb: already
从	cóng	Relative Clause: from
到	dào	Verb: to arrive, to reach Relative Clause: to, until, up to
远	yuǎn	Adjective: far, distant
离	lí	Verb: to leave, to be away from

近	jìn	Adjective: near, close
出	chū	Verb: to go out, to exceed, to happen Measure Word: for dramas, plays, operas
进	jìn	Verb: to advance, to enter
外	wài	Adjective: foreign, external Location: outside
旁边	páng biān	Location: beside, aside
右边	yòu bian	Location: right, right side
左边	zuǒ bian	Location: left, left side
两	liǎng	Number: two, some Measure Word: 50 gram
每	měi	Adverb: each, per Pronoun: all, each, every
第一	dì yī	Number: first, number one
百	bǎi	Number: 100
千	qiān	Number: 1000
快	kuài	Adjective: quick, rapid Adverb: soon, almost
慢	màn	Adjective: slow
起床	qǐ chuáng	Verb: to get up (from bed)
早上	zǎo shang	Time: early morning
晚上	wǎn shang	Time: evening
去年	qù nián	Time: last year
就	jiù	Adverb: only, already Relative Clause: with regard to Conjunction: as soon as, right away, even if
时间	shí jiān	Noun: time, period
长	cháng	Noun: length Adjective: long
小时	xiǎo shí	Noun: hour
还	hái	Adverb: still
等	děng	Verb: to wait
次	cì	Noun: order, sequence Measure Word: "time(s)"

再	zài	Adverb: again, once more
贵	guì	Adjective: expensive
便宜	pián yi	Adjective: cheap, inexpensive
卖	mài	Verb: to sell
件	jiàn	Measure Word: for events, things, clothes, etc.
西瓜	xī guā	Noun: watermelon
咖啡	kā fēi	Noun: coffee
服务员	fú wù yuán	Noun: waiter, service personnel
鸡蛋	jī dàn	Noun: (chicken) egg
牛奶	niú nǎi	Noun: cow milk
羊肉	yáng ròu	Noun: mutton
鱼	yú	Noun: fish
好吃	hǎo chī	Adjective: tasty, delicious
新	xīn	Adjective: new
颜色	yán sè	Noun: colour
白	bái	Adjective: white, blank Adverb: free of charge, for nothing
黑	hēi	Adjective: black, dark
红	hóng	Noun: dividend Adjective: red, popular, revolutionary
公共汽车	gōng gòng qì chē	Noun: bus
机场	jī chǎng	Noun: airport
零	líng	Number: 0
走	zǒu	Verb: to walk
路	lù	Noun: road, path
票	piào	Noun: ticket
面条	miàn tiáo	Noun: noodles
旅游	lǚ yóu	Noun: trip, journey Verb: to travel
可以	kě yǐ	Auxiliary Verb: can, may, able to

可能	kě néng	Adverb: might, maybe Auxiliary Verb: can
哥哥	gē ge	Noun: older brother
弟弟	dì di	Noun: younger brother
姐姐	jiě jie	Noun: older sister
妹妹	mèi mei	Noun: younger sister
妻子	qī zi	Noun: wife
日	rì	Noun: day, sun
丈夫	zhàng fu	Noun: husband
生日	shēng rì	Noun: birthday
快乐	kuài lè	Adjective: happy
孩子	hái zi	Noun: child
姓	xìng	Noun: surname
唱歌	chàng gē	Verb: to sing
送	sòng	Verb: to deliver, to escort, to give, to send
给	gěi	Verb: to give
笑	xiào	Verb: to smile, to laugh
教室	jiào shì	Noun: classroom
课	kè	Noun: class, lesson, course
考试	kǎo shì	Noun: exam
休息	xiū xi	Noun: rest Verb: to rest
问题	wèn tí	Noun: problem, question
意思	yì si	Noun: meaning, opinion, idea
门	mén	Noun: door Measure Word: for lessons
对	duì	Adjective: right, correct
错	cuò	Noun: mistake, error Adjective: wrong
问	wèn	Verb: to ask
铅笔	qiān bǐ	Noun: pencil

题	tí	Noun: question (of a test) Verb: to inscribe, to mention
懂	dǒng	Verb: to understand, to know
希望	xī wàng	Noun: hope Verb: to hope, to wish
准备	zhǔn bèi	Verb: to prepare
帮助	bāng zhù	Noun: assistance, help Verb: to help, to assist
雪	xuě	Noun: snow
阴	yīn	Adjective: cloudy, overcast
晴	qíng	Adjective: clear, sunny
身体	shēn tǐ	Noun: body, health
眼睛	yǎn jing	Noun: eye
药	yào	Noun: medicine, drug
生病	shēng bìng	Verb: to get sick
穿	chuān	Verb: to wear
洗	xǐ	Verb: to wash
忙	máng	Adjective: busy
累	lèi	Adjective: tired
上班	shàng bān	Verb: to go to work, to start work
火车站	huǒ chē zhàn	Noun: train station
报纸	bào zhǐ	Noun: newspaper
公司	gōng sī	Noun: company
房间	fáng jiān	Noun: room
事情	shì qing	Noun: thing, affair, matter
手表	shǒu biǎo	Noun: wrist watch
手机	shǒu jī	Noun: mobile phone
别	bié	Verb: to leave, to distinguish Adjective: other, another Adverb: don't
真	zhēn	Adverb: real, true, genuine

开始	kāi shǐ	Noun: beginning Verb: to begin
知道	zhī dào	Verb: to know, to be aware of
找	zhǎo	Verb: to look for, to seek
介绍	jiè shào	Noun: introduction Verb: to introduce, to recommend
告诉	gào su	Verb: to tell
运动	yùn dòng	Noun: movement, sports Verb: to move about
跑步	pǎo bù	Verb: to run
打篮球	dǎ lán qiú	Verb: play basketball
踢足球	tī zú qiú	Verb: to play football
跳舞	tiào wǔ	Verb: to dance
游泳	yóu yǒng	Noun: swimming Verb: to swim
玩	wán	Verb: to play, to have fun
觉得	jué de	Verb: to think, to feel
完	wán	Verb: to finish
也	yě	Adverb: also
说话	shuō huà	Verb: to speak, to talk, to gossip
高	gāo	Adjective: high, tall
让	ràng	Verb: to permit, to let sbd. do sth.
宾馆	bīn guǎn	Noun: hotel

HSK 3

词典	cí diǎn	Noun: dictionary
只	zhī	Measure Word: for birds and animals, a pair of things, parts of the body, etc.
感兴趣	gǎn xìng qù	Verb: to be interested in
笔记本	bǐ jì běn	Noun: notebook
试	shì	Noun: experiment, examination, test Verb: to test, to attempt
中文	Zhōng wén	Noun: Chinese language
皮鞋	pí xié	Noun: leather shoes
个子	gè zi	Noun: height, stature
瓶子	píng zi	Noun: bottle
不但 x 而且 y	bù dàn x ér qiě y	Conjunction: not only x but also y
黄河	huáng hé	Noun: Yellow River
热情	rè qíng	Adjective: cordial, passionate
饮料	yǐn liào	Noun: drink, beverage
只有 x 才 y	zhǐ yǒu x cái y	Conjunction: only if x then y
起飞	qǐ fēi	Verb: to take off
起来	qǐ lái	Verb: to stand up, to get up
聊天	liáo tiān	Verb: to chat
留学	liú xué	Verb: to study abroad
嘴	zuǐ	Noun: mouth
最后	zuì hòu	Time: finally, at last
请假	qǐng jià	Verb: to ask for leave
过	guò	Verb: to pass, to cross, to spend time
发	fā	Verb: to send out, to issue, to develop Measure Word: for gunshots
信用卡	xìn yòng kǎ	Noun: credit card
后来	hòu lái	Adverb: afterwards, later

把	bǎ	Noun: handle Verb: to grasp, to hold Particle: for ba-sentences Measure Word: for a bunch or objects with handle
放	fàng	Verb: to let go, to put, have a vacation
被	bèi	Relative Clause: by (for passive sentence)
如果	rú guǒ	Conjunction: if
还是	hái shì	Adverb: still, nevertheless Conjunction: or
或者	huò zhě	Conjunction: or, possibly
突然	tū rán	Adjective: sudden, abrupt Adverb: suddenly, unexpectedly
除了	chú le	Conjunction: except for, apart from, besides
先	xiān	Adverb: early, former, first, before
然后	rán hòu	Conjunction: then, afterwards
其实	qí shí	Adverb: actually, in fact
地	de	Particle: used before a verb
关于	guān yú	Relative Clause: concerning, with regards to, about
终于	zhōng yú	Adverb: at last, finally, eventually
当然	dāng rán	Adverb: certainly, of course
刚才	gāng cái	Time: just a moment ago
以前	yǐ qián	Time: before Adverb: previous, formerly
一样	yí yàng	Adverb: alike, equal to
一直	yī zhí	Adverb: always, continuously, straight
一会儿	yí huì r	Time: a while Adverb: in a moment, a little while
一般	yì bān	Adjective: ordinary, general, common Adverb: in general, generally
一边	yì biān	Location: one side Adverb: on the one hand
一定	yí dìng	Adjective: definite, fixed, given Adverb: surely, certainly
一共	yí gòng	Adverb: altogether

草	cǎo	Noun: grass, straw
动物	dòng wù	Noun: animal
向	xiàng	Noun: direction Verb: to face, to turn towards Adverb: formerly, all along Relative Clause: towards
花	huā	Noun: flower
花	huā	Verb: to spend
马	mǎ	Noun: horse
马上	mǎ shàng	Adverb: immediately, at once
鸟	niǎo	Noun: bird
骑	qí	Verb: to ride (animal or bike)
元	yuán	Measure Word: for money (Yuan, RMB)
树	shù	Noun: tree
比较	bǐ jiào	Adverb: quite, rather, fairly, comparatively
熊猫	xióng māo	Noun: panda
更	gèng	Adverb: even more
坏	huài	Adjective: bad, broken, spoiled
特别	tè bié	Adjective: special, particular
发现	fā xiàn	Verb: to discover, to find
多么	duō me	Adverb: how, what
用	yòng	Verb: to use, to employ, to apply
又	yòu	Adverb: again
越	yuè	Verb: to exceed, to climb over, to surpass
只	zhǐ	Adverb: only, just, merely
种	zhǒng	Noun: species, race, breed Measure Word: type, kind, sort or for languages
中间	zhōng jiān	Location: between, in the middle, mid
锻炼	duàn liàn	Verb: to exercise, to engage in physical exercise
矮	ǎi	Adjective: low, short

鼻子	bí zi	Noun: nose
耳朵	ěr duo	Noun: ear
公斤	gōng jīn	Noun: kilogram Measure Word: kg
发烧	fā shāo	Verb: to have fever
感冒	gǎn mào	Noun: common cold Verb: to catch a cold
健康	jiàn kāng	Noun: health Adjective: healthy
脚	jiǎo	Noun: foot
脸	liǎn	Noun: face
头发	tóu fa	Noun: hair (on the head)
腿	tuǐ	Noun: leg
胖	pàng	Adjective: fat, plump
瘦	shòu	Adjective: thin, slim
欢迎	huān yíng	Expression: welcome!
口	kǒu	Noun: mouth Measure Word: for things with mouths or a mouth full of
根据	gēn jù	Noun: basis, foundation Verb: to base on Relative Clause: according to, based on
饱	bǎo	Adjective: full (from eating)
菜单	cài dān	Noun: menu
蛋糕	dàn gāo	Noun: cake
自行车	zì xíng chē	Noun: bicycle, bike
饿	è	Adjective: hungry
船	chuán	Noun: boat, ship
渴	kě	Adjective: thirsty
筷子	kuài zi	Noun: chopsticks
米	mǐ	Noun: rice Measure Word: for metre
面包	miàn bāo	Noun: bread

张	zhāng	Verb: to open up, to spread Measure Word: for pieces, flat objects
盘子	pán zi	Noun: tray, plate, dish
啤酒	pí jiǔ	Noun: beer
碗	wǎn	Noun: bowl
香蕉	xiāng jiāo	Noun: banana
新鲜	xīn xiān	Adjective: fresh (food, experience, etc.)
冰箱	bīng xiāng	Noun: fridge, icebox
甜	tián	Adjective: sweet
啊	a	Particle: showing approval
班	bān	Noun: class, team, squad Measure Word: for groups, rankings, etc.
迟到	chí dào	Verb: to be late
聪明	cōng ming	Adjective: clever, intelligent, smart
复习	fù xí	Noun: revision Verb: to revise
黑板	hēi bǎn	Noun: blackboard
简单	jiǎn dān	Adjective: simple, uncomplicated
教	jiāo	Verb: to teach, to instruct
借	jiè	Verb: to lend, to borrow, to make use of (an opportunity)
句子	jù zi	Noun: sentence
历史	lì shǐ	Noun: history
练习	liàn xí	Noun: exercise, practice Verb: to practice
了解	liǎo jiě	Verb: to understand
明白	míng bai	Verb: to understand Adjective: clear, obvious
难	nán	Adjective: difficult
努力	nǔ lì	Noun: great effort Verb: to strive, to work/study hard Adjective: hard, hardworking
年级	nián jí	Noun: grade, year
认真	rèn zhēn	Adjective: conscientious, earnest, serious

容易	róng yì	Adjective: easy
数学	shù xué	Noun: mathematics
回答	huí dá	Noun: answer Verb: to answer, to reply
水平	shuǐ píng	Noun: level, standard Adjective: horizontal
提高	tí gāo	Verb: to raise, to increase
图书馆	tú shū guǎn	Noun: library
校长	xiào zhǎng	Noun: headmaster, president (university)
要求	yāo qiú	Noun: demand, requirement Verb: to require, to demand
作业	zuò yè	Noun: homework, task, work
成绩	chéng jì	Noun: score, achievement, grades
记得	jì de	Verb: to remember
差	chà	Verb: to lack, short of Adjective: poor
段	duàn	Measure Word: for paragraphs, segments, periods, stories
长	zhǎng	Verb: to grow, to develop
节目	jié mù	Noun: program, item
经过	jīng guò	Verb: to pass, to go through Relative Clause: after, as a result of
包	bāo	Noun: bag, package Verb: to cover, to wrap, to hold, to include
超市	chāo shì	Noun: supermarket
衬衫	chèn shān	Noun: shirt, blouse
帽子	mào zi	Noun: hat, cap
带	dài	Noun: band, belt, area, region Verb: to wear, to carry, to bring, to lead
分	fēn	Noun: minute, point, 0.01 Yuan Verb: to divide, to distinguish
换	huàn	Verb: to change, to exchange
礼物	lǐ wù	Noun: gift, present
裙子	qún zi	Noun: skirt

伞	sǎn	Noun: umbrella
上网	shàng wǎng	Verb: to go on the internet
舒服	shū fu	Adjective: comfortable
忘记	wàng jì	Verb: to forget
选择	xuǎn zé	Noun: choice, option Verb: to choose, to select
照相机	zhào xiàng jī	Noun: camera
周末	zhōu mò	Noun: weekend
关	guān	Noun: mountain pass, barrier Verb: to close, to shut, to turn off
双	shuāng	Adjective: two, pair, both Measure Word: for a pair (of shoes, etc.)
条	tiáo	Noun: strip, clause Measure Word: for long thin things
拿	ná	Verb: to hold, to seize
爱好	ài hào	Noun: hobby, interest Verb: to like
比赛	bǐ sài	Noun: competition, match Verb: to compete
画	huà	Noun: picture, painting Verb: to draw, to paint
客人	kè rén	Noun: guest, customer, visitor
老	lǎo	Adjective: old Adverb: always
年轻	nián qīng	Adjective: young
爬山	pá shān	Noun: hiking Verb: to climb a mountain
体育	tǐ yù	Noun: sports
照顾	zhào gù	Verb: to take care of, to look after
音乐	yīn yuè	Noun: music
游戏	yóu xì	Noun: game, play
决定	jué dìng	Noun: decision Verb: to decide
奇怪	qí guài	Adjective: strange, weird
其他	qí tā	Pronoun: other, others

几乎	jī hū	Adverb: almost, nearly
办法	bàn fǎ	Noun: method, way, means
办公室	bàn gōng shì	Noun: office, bureau
帮忙	bāng máng	Verb: to help, to do a favour
参加	cān jiā	Verb: to attend, to take part, to join
层	céng	Noun: layer, floor Measure Word: for layer, story, floor
电子邮件	diàn zǐ yóu jiàn	Noun: email
护照	hù zhào	Noun: passport
会议	huì yì	Noun: meeting, conference
机会	jī huì	Noun: opportunity, chance
检查	jiǎn chá	Noun: inspection Verb: to check, to inspect, to examine
讲	jiǎng	Noun: speech, lecture Verb: to speak, to explain, to negotiate
解决	jiě jué	Verb: to settle (dispute), to resolve, to solve
节日	jié rì	Noun: holiday, festival
经理	jīng lǐ	Noun: manager, director
满意	mǎn yì	Verb: to satisfy Adjective: satisfied
清楚	qīng chu	Adjective: clear, distinct
认为	rèn wéi	Verb: to think, to believe, to consider
同事	tóng shì	Noun: colleague
万	wàn	Number: 10000
行李箱	xíng li xiāng	Noun: suitcase
关系	guān xì	Noun: relationship, relation Verb: to affect, to have to do with
同意	tóng yì	Verb: to agree, to consent, to approve
完成	wán chéng	Verb: to complete, to accomplish
位	wèi	Noun: position, place, seat Measure Word: for people
为了	wèi le	Relative Clause: for, in order to
新闻	xīn wén	Noun: news

需要	xū yào	Noun: needs Verb: to need, to want
必须	bì xū	Auxiliary Verb: to have to, to must
应该	yīng gāi	Auxiliary Verb: should, ought to
结束	jié shù	Noun: termination, end Verb: to finish, to end, to conclude
旧	jiù	Adjective: old, used, worn
为	wèi	Verb: to do, to act, to be, to become Relative Clause: for (sbd.)
重要	zhòng yào	Adjective: important
注意	zhù yì	Verb: to pay attention to
主要	zhǔ yào	Adjective: main, principal, major
城市	chéng shì	Noun: city, town
安静	ān jìng	Adjective: quiet, peaceful
北方	běi fāng	Location: north, northern part of a country
南	nán	Location: south
西	xī	Location: west
东	dōng	Location: east
地方	dì fang	Noun: region, place, location
地铁	dì tiě	Noun: subway
地图	dì tú	Noun: map
干净	gān jìng	Adjective: clean, tidy
公园	gōng yuán	Noun: park
刮风	guā fēng	Verb: to be windy
环境	huán jìng	Noun: environment, surroundings
接	jiē	Verb: to receive, to meet, to connect, to catch
街道	jiē dào	Noun: street
辆	liàng	Measure Word: for vehicles
司机	sī jī	Noun: driver
文化	wén huà	Noun: culture
国家	guó jiā	Noun: country, state, nation

银行	yín háng	Noun: bank (for money)
站	zhàn	Noun: station, stop Verb: to stand, to stop, to halt
有名	yǒu míng	Adjective: famous, well known
搬	bān	Verb: to move, to shift
打扫	dǎ sǎo	Verb: to clean
灯	dēng	Noun: lamp, light
电梯	diàn tī	Noun: elevator
方便	fāng biàn	Adjective: convenient
附近	fù jìn	Noun: vicinity Adverb: nearby Relative Clause: next to
角	jiǎo	Noun: angle, corner, horn Measure Word: for 0.1 yuan
空调	kōng tiáo	Noun: air conditioning
裤子	kù zi	Noun: trousers
邻居	lín jū	Noun: neighbour
楼	lóu	Noun: storied building Measure Word: for floor
声音	shēng yīn	Noun: voice, sound
洗手间	xǐ shǒu jiān	Noun: toilet, bathroom
洗澡	xǐ zǎo	Verb: to take a shower, to have a bath
刷牙	shuā yá	Verb: to brush teeth
照片	zhào piàn	Noun: photo, picture
自己	zì jǐ	Pronoun: oneself, self
总是	zǒng shì	Adverb: always
离开	lí kāi	Verb: to depart, to leave
春	chūn	Noun: spring
打算	dǎ suàn	Noun: plan, intention Verb: to plan, to think of, to calculate
冬	dōng	Noun: winter
短	duǎn	Adjective: short, brief

半	bàn	Number: half
季节	jì jié	Noun: season, period
久	jiǔ	Adjective: long (time)
极	jí	Noun: pole Adverb: extremely, highly
秋	qiū	Noun: autumn, fall
世界	shì jiè	Noun: world
太阳	tài yáng	Noun: sun
月亮	yuè liang	Noun: moon
夏	xià	Noun: summer
蓝	lán	Adjective: blue
绿	lǜ	Adjective: green
变化	biàn huà	Noun: change, variation
阿姨	ā yí	Noun: aunt
叔叔	shū shu	Noun: uncle
故事	gù shi	Noun: story, tale
结婚	jié hūn	Noun: marriage, wedding Verb: to marry
可爱	kě ài	Adjective: cute, lovely
哭	kū	Verb: to cry, to weep
奶奶	nǎi nai	Noun: grandmother (father's mother)
爷爷	yé ye	Noun: grandfather (father's father)
影响	yǐng xiǎng	Noun: influence, effect Verb: to influence, to affect
别人	bié ren	Pronoun: others, other people
跟	gēn	Verb: to follow Relative Clause: with Conjunction: and
还	huán	Verb: to give back, to return
见面	jiàn miàn	Verb: to meet, to see sbd.
经常	jīng cháng	Adverb: often, frequently

刻	kè	Verb: to cut, to carve Measure Word: for quarter of an hour
习惯	xí guàn	Noun: habit, usual practice, custom Verb: to be/get used to
像	xiàng	Verb: be/look like, to appear, to seem
担心	dān xīn	Verb: to worry Adjective: worried, anxious
放心	fàng xīn	Verb: to rest, to be at ease
关心	guān xīn	Noun: concern Verb: to care for
害怕	hài pà	Verb: to be afraid, to fear
难过	nán guò	Verb: to feel sorry, sad
生气	shēng qì	Verb: to be/get angry Adjective: angry, mad
疼	téng	Noun: pain Verb: to ache, to hurt
小心	xiǎo xīn	Verb: to be careful Adjective: careful Expression: Take care!
相信	xiāng xìn	Verb: to believe in, have faith in
愿意	yuàn yì	Auxiliary Verb: to be willing, be ready, to wish, to want
着急	zháo jí	Verb: to worry, to be nervous
最近	zuì jìn	Adverb: recently, lately, soon
遇到	yù dào	Verb: to meet, to run into
过去	guò qù	Verb: to go over, to pass by Adverb: past, former

出生	chū shēng	Verb: to be born
护士	hù shi	Noun: nurse
提前	tí qián	Verb: to bring forward Adjective: early Adverb: beforehand
入口	rù kǒu	Noun: entrance
提醒	tí xǐng	Verb: to remind, to call attention to
互相	hù xiāng	Adverb: each other
爱情	ài qíng	Noun: love
份	fèn	Noun: part, share, portion, copy Measure Word: for newspaper, papers, reports, contracts
目的	mù dì	Noun: purpose, aim
招聘	zhāo pìn	Noun: recruitment Verb: to recruit
母亲	mǔ qīn	Noun: mother
填空	tián kòng	Verb: to fill in (questionnaire, etc.)
传真	chuán zhēn	Noun: fax
散步	sàn bù	Verb: to take/to go for a walk
作家	zuò jiā	Noun: author
安排	ān pái	Noun: plan Verb: to plan, to arrange
窗户	chuāng hu	Noun: window
森林	sēn lín	Noun: forest
安全	ān quán	Noun: safety Adjective: safe, secure
按时	àn shí	Adjective: on time, on schedule
开玩笑	kāi wán xiào	Verb: to play a joke, to make fun of
开心	kāi xīn	Verb: to feel happy, to make fun of sbd. Adjective: happy
沙发	shā fā	Noun: sofa
条件	tiáo jiàn	Noun: condition, circumstances

按照	àn zhào	Relative Clause: according to
耐心	nài xīn	Noun: patience Adjective: patient
丰富	fēng fù	Adjective: rich, plentiful
怀疑	huái yí	Noun: doubt, suspicion Verb: to doubt, to suspect
看法	kàn fǎ	Noun: view, opinion
难道	nán dào	Adverb: don't tell me ..., is it possible that ...
许多	xǔ duō	Adjective: many, a lot of
挺	tǐng	Verb: to stick out, to stand straight Adverb: quite, very, rather Measure Word: for machine guns
真正	zhēn zhèng	Adjective: genuine, real, true
考虑	kǎo lǜ	Noun: consideration Verb: to think over, to consider
难受	nán shòu	Verb: to be difficult to bear
正常	zhèng cháng	Adjective: regular, normal, ordinary
烤鸭	kǎo yā	Noun: roast duck
通过	tōng guò	Verb: to pass through, to get through Relative Clause: via, by
否则	fǒu zé	Conjunction: otherwise
内	nèi	Location: inside, inner
正好	zhèng hǎo	Adverb: just right, just at the right time
从来	cóng lái	Adverb: always, ever since, at all times
商量	shāng liang	Verb: to consult, to discuss
同情	tóng qíng	Noun: sympathy, compassion Verb: to sympathize
富	fù	Adjective: rich
内容	nèi róng	Noun: content, substance
同时	tóng shí	Time: at the same time, simultaneously
学期	xué qī	Noun: term, semester
棵	kē	Measure Word: for trees, plants, etc.
整理	zhěng lǐ	Verb: to arrange, to tidy up

符合	fú hé	Verb: to accord with, to conform to
伤心	shāng xīn	Adjective: sad, grievous, broken-hearted
证明	zhèng míng	Noun: proof, certificate, testimonial Verb: to prove, to testify
棒	bàng	Noun: stick, club Adjective: strong, capable, good Measure Word: for legs of relay race
能力	néng lì	Noun: ability, capability
付款	fù kuǎn	Noun: payment Verb: to pay
稍微	shāo wēi	Adverb: a little bit
粗心	cū xīn	Adjective: careless, thoughtless
父亲	fù qīn	Noun: father
勺子	sháo zi	Noun: spoon
通知	tōng zhī	Noun: notice Verb: to notify, to inform
正确	zhèng què	Adjective: correct, proper
抱	bào	Verb: to hug, to embrace, to hold
存	cún	Verb: to deposit, to keep
正式	zhèng shì	Adjective: formal, official
复印	fù yìn	Verb: to (photo)copy
可怜	kě lián	Adjective: pitiful, poor, pathetic
呀	ya	Particle: expressing surprise or doubt
复杂	fù zá	Adjective: complicated, complex
社会	shè huì	Noun: society
牙膏	yá gāo	Noun: toothpaste
负责	fù zé	Verb: to be responsible for
回忆	huí yì	Noun: recollection Verb: to recall, to recollect
年龄	nián líng	Noun: age (of a person)
压力	yā lì	Noun: pressure
错误	cuò wù	Noun: error, mistake

亚洲	Yà zhōu	Noun: Asia
可是	kě shì	Conjunction: but
盐	yán	Noun: salt
刚	gāng	Adverb: just, barely
答案	dá àn	Noun: answer, solution
咳嗽	ké sou	Noun: cough Verb: to cough
指	zhǐ	Noun: finger Verb: to point at or to, to indicate
打扮	dǎ ban	Verb: to decorate, to dress up
改变	gǎi biàn	Verb: to change
火	huǒ	Noun: fire
客厅	kè tīng	Noun: living room
演出	yǎn chū	Noun: performance, show Verb: to perform, to put on a show
之	zhī	Pronoun: I, he, she it, ... Particle: to form an attribute
可惜	kě xī	Adjective: it is a pity, what a pity
严格	yán gé	Adjective: strict, rigorous
科学	kē xué	Noun: science Adjective: scientific
深	shēn	Adjective: deep, dark (colour, etc.)
支持	zhī chí	Noun: support, backing Verb: to support, to back
保护	bǎo hù	Noun: protection Verb: to protect, to safeguard
大概	dà gài	Adverb: probably, roughly
获得	huò dé	Verb: to obtain, to acquire
肯定	kěn dìng	Verb: to affirm, to confirm Adjective: certain, definite Adverb: certainly, definitely
弄	nòng	Verb: to do, to make
活动	huó dòng	Noun: activity Verb: to move about Adjective: active

推	tuī	Verb: to push
活泼	huó pō	Adjective: lively, vivid
值得	zhí dé	Verb: to be worth, to deserve
报名	bào míng	Verb: to sign up, to register
干	gàn	Verb: to do, to work
恐怕	kǒng pà	Adverb: I'm afraid that...
推迟	tuī chí	Verb: to postpone, to defer
抱歉	bào qiàn	Expression: sorry! my apologies!
空气	kōng qì	Noun: air, atmosphere
演员	yǎn yuán	Noun: performer, actor
干杯	gān bēi	Expression: Cheers!
严重	yán zhòng	Adjective: grave, serious, critical
只好	zhǐ hǎo	Adverb: have to
保证	bǎo zhèng	Noun: guarantee Verb: to guarantee, to ensure, to assure
打扰	dǎ rǎo	Verb: to disturb
寄	jì	Verb: to send, to mail
感动	gǎn dòng	Verb: to move sbd., to be moved
申请	shēn qǐng	Noun: application Verb: to apply for
养成	yǎng chéng	Verb: to cultivate, to form, to acquire
包子	bāo zi	Noun: steamed stuffed bun
大使馆	dà shǐ guǎn	Noun: embassy
暖和	nuǎn huo	Adjective: warm
脱	tuō	Verb: to take off, to shed
阳光	yáng guāng	Noun: sunshine
直接	zhí jiē	Adjective: direct, immediate
偶尔	ǒu ěr	Adverb: occasionally
甚至	shèn zhì	Adverb: even
袜子	wà zi	Noun: socks, stockings

倍	bèi	Measure Word: for times, -fold
基础	jī chǔ	Noun: base, foundation, basis
苦	kǔ	Adjective: bitter, miserable
剩	shèng	Verb: to remain
质量	zhì liàng	Noun: quality
省	shěng	Noun: province Verb: to save, to omit
感觉	gǎn jué	Noun: feeling, sense Verb: to feel
样子	yàng zi	Noun: appearance, manner
打印	dǎ yìn	Verb: to print, to seal, to stamp
激动	jī dòng	Verb: to excite Adjective: exciting
至少	zhì shǎo	Adverb: at least
排队	pái duì	Verb: to queue, to line up
知识	zhī shi	Noun: knowledge
大约	dà yuē	Adverb: approximately
感情	gǎn qíng	Noun: emotion, feeling
排列	pái liè	Noun: arrangement, permutation Verb: to arrange, to put in order
植物	zhí wù	Noun: plant
打招呼	dǎ zhāo hu	Verb: to greet sbd., to give prior notice
打折	dǎ zhé	Verb: to give discount
计划	jì huà	Noun: plan, project, program Verb: to plan
判断	pàn duàn	Noun: decision, judgement Verb: to decide, to judge
生活	shēng huó	Noun: life Verb: to live
笨	bèn	Adjective: stupid, foolish
打针	dǎ zhēn	Verb: to inject
感谢	gǎn xiè	Noun: gratitude Verb: to thank, to be grateful
只要	zhǐ yào	Conjunction: if only, as long as

积极	jī jí	Adjective: positive, active
邀请	yāo qǐng	Noun: invitation Verb: to invite
职业	zhí yè	Noun: occupation, profession
戴	dài	Verb: to put on, to wear, to respect, to support
矿泉水	kuàng quán shuǐ	Noun: mineral water
生命	shēng mìng	Noun: life
本来	běn lái	Adjective: original Adverb: originally, at first
积累	jī lěi	Noun: accumulation Verb: to accumulate
困	kùn	Adjective: sleepy, tired
完全	wán quán	Adjective: complete, whole, entire
钥匙	yào shi	Noun: key
困难	kùn nan	Noun: difficulty, problem Adjective: difficult
要是	yào shi	Conjunction: if, in case
大夫	dài fu	Noun: doctor
陪	péi	Verb: to accompany
页	yè	Noun: page, leaf Measure Word: for a page
辣	là	Adjective: spicy
拉	lā	Verb: to pull
重	zhòng	Adjective: heavy, serious Adverb: heavily
赶	gǎn	Verb: to hurry to do sth.
垃圾桶	lā jī tǒng	Noun: rubbish bin
也许	yě xǔ	Adverb: perhaps, maybe
重点	zhòng diǎn	Noun: emphasis, focal point, priority
高速公路	gāo sù gōng lù	Noun: highway
网球	wǎng qiú	Noun: tennis
来不及	lái bu jí	Verb: there's not enough time

失败	shī bài	Noun: defeat, failure Verb: to lose, to be defeated
往往	wǎng wǎng	Adverb: often
来得及	lái de jí	Verb: there is still time to do sth.
网站	wǎng zhàn	Noun: website
叶子	yè zi	Noun: leaf
比如	bǐ rú	Adverb: for example
各	gè	Pronoun: each, every
既然	jì rán	Conjunction: this being the case
来自	lái zì	Verb: to come from
以	yǐ	Relative Clause: because of, so as to, in order to
重视	zhòng shì	Verb: to value, to attach importance to
及时	jí shí	Adjective: in time Adverb: without delay
皮肤	pí fū	Noun: skin
胳膊	gē bo	Noun: arm
即使	jí shǐ	Conjunction: even if, even though
十分	shí fēn	Adverb: very, completely, fully, utterly, absolutely
技术	jì shù	Noun: technology, skill, technique
懒	lǎn	Adjective: lazy
是否	shì fǒu	Conjunction: whether (or not)
毕业	bì yè	Verb: to graduate, to finish school
批评	pī píng	Noun: criticism Verb: to criticize
师傅	shī fu	Noun: master, teacher, used to respectfully address older men
浪费	làng fèi	Verb: to waste
脾气	pí qi	Noun: temperament, temper
适合	shì hé	Verb: to fit, to suit
遍	biàn	Adverb: all over Measure Word: for a time

继续	jì xù	Noun: continuation Verb: to continue, to go on
浪漫	làng màn	Adjective: romantic
当	dāng	Verb: to act as, to administer Auxiliary Verb: should, ought Adjective: equal Conjunction: when, during
味道	wèi dào	Noun: taste, flavour
记者	jì zhě	Noun: reporter, journalist
骗	piàn	Verb: to cheat, to swindle
实际	shí jì	Noun: reality, practice Adjective: realistic, practical
世纪	shì jì	Noun: century
周围	zhōu wéi	Noun: surroundings, environment Adverb: around, about
篇	piān	Measure Word: for chapters, articles, etc.
当时	dāng shí	Time: at that time, then
假	jiǎ	Adjective: fake, false
老虎	lǎo hǔ	Noun: tiger
倒	dào	Verb: to pour, to reverse Adverb: on the contrary, instead
表格	biǎo gé	Noun: form, table
加班	jiā bān	Verb: to work overtime
刀	dāo	Noun: knife
意见	yì jiàn	Noun: opinion, view, objection
旅行	lǚ xíng	Noun: journey Verb: to travel
到处	dào chù	Adverb: everywhere, at all places
价格	jià gé	Noun: price
家具	jiā jù	Noun: furniture
卫生间	wèi shēng jiān	Noun: bathroom, WC
到底	dào dǐ	Adverb: finally, in the end
危险	wēi xiǎn	Noun: danger Adjective: dangerous

表扬	biǎo yáng	Verb: to praise, to commend
功夫	gōng fu	Noun: time, skill, labour, workmanship, kung fu
祝贺	zhù hè	Noun: congratulations Verb: to congratulate
道歉	dào qiàn	Verb: to apologize
标准	biāo zhǔn	Noun: standard, norm Adjective: standard
加油站	jiā yóu zhàn	Noun: gas station
冷静	lěng jìng	Adjective: calm, cool-headed, quiet
一切	yí qiè	Pronoun: all, everything
著名	zhù míng	Adjective: famous, well-known
导游	dǎo yóu	Noun: tour guide
公里	gōng lǐ	Noun: kilometre Measure Word: for km
失望	shī wàng	Noun: disappointment Verb: to lose hope Adjective: disappointed
艺术	yì shù	Noun: art
礼拜天	lǐ bài tiān	Time: Sunday
乒乓球	pīng pāng qiú	Noun: table tennis
温度	wēn dù	Noun: temperature
主意	zhǔ yi	Noun: idea, plan, decision
饼干	bǐng gān	Noun: biscuit, cookie
得意	dé yì	Adjective: pleased with oneself
理发	lǐ fà	Verb: to have a haircut
平时	píng shí	Noun: in peacetime Adverb: normally
并且	bìng qiě	Conjunction: and, besides, moreover
得	děi	Auxiliary Verb: to have to
共同	gòng tóng	Adjective: common, joint, together
厉害	lì hai	Adjective: awesome, terrible, strict, severe, difficult to deal with

破	pò	Verb: to break, to destroy Adjective: broken, damaged
等	děng	Particle: etc., and so on
坚持	jiān chí	Verb: to stick to, to persist in, to insist on
赚	zhuàn	Verb: to earn, to make a profit
博士	bó shì	Noun: doctor, Ph.D.
理解	lǐ jiě	Noun: comprehension, understanding Verb: to comprehend, to understand
减肥	jiǎn féi	Verb: to lose weight
普遍	pǔ biàn	Adjective: universal, general
适应	shì yìng	Verb: to fit, to suit, to adapt
专门	zhuān mén	Adjective: special, specialized Adverb: specialized
登机牌	dēng jī pái	Noun: boarding pass
使用	shǐ yòng	Verb: to use
工资	gōng zī	Noun: salary, wages
实在	shí zài	Adjective: real, true Adverb: really, in fact
文章	wén zhāng	Noun: article, essay
专业	zhuān yè	Noun: speciality, major, field of study
礼貌	lǐ mào	Noun: politeness, courtesy
底	dǐ	Noun: background, end, bottom, base
够	gòu	Verb: to reach, to be enough Adjective: be enough Adverb: enough
因此	yīn cǐ	Conjunction: thus, consequently
力气	lì qi	Noun: strength
不得不	bù dé bù	Auxiliary Verb: to have to, cannot but
例如	lì rú	Adverb: for example
其次	qí cì	Adverb: next, secondary Conjunction: secondly
收	shōu	Verb: to accept, to receive
无	wú	Adverb: not

购物	gòu wù	Verb: to go shopping
受不了	shòu bù liǎo	Adjective: unbearable
引起	yǐn qǐ	Verb: to give rise to, to lead to
百分之	bǎi fēn zhī	Noun: percent
部分	bù fen	Noun: part, section
受到	shòu dào	Verb: to receive, to suffer
左右	zuǒ yòu	Adverb: about, approximately, around
不管	bù guǎn	Conjunction: regardless of, no matter what/how
减少	jiǎn shǎo	Verb: to reduce, to decrease
首都	shǒu dū	Noun: capital city
误会	wù huì	Noun: misunderstanding Verb: to misunderstand
准确	zhǔn què	Adjective: accurate, precise, exact
不过	bú guò	Adverb: only, just, no more than Conjunction: but, however
地球	dì qiú	Noun: earth (planet)
理想	lǐ xiǎng	Noun: ideal, dream
印象	yìn xiàng	Noun: impression
准时	zhǔn shí	Adjective: on time, punctual
气候	qì hòu	Noun: climate, atmosphere
无聊	wú liáo	Adjective: boring, bored
建议	jiàn yì	Noun: suggestion Verb: to suggest
售货员	shòu huò yuán	Noun: salesperson
无论	wú lùn	Conjunction: no matter how/what
赢	yíng	Verb: to win, to beat
不仅	bù jǐn	Conjunction: not only, not just
估计	gū jì	Verb: to estimate
顾客	gù kè	Noun: client, customer
俩	liǎ	Number: two (people)

连	lián	Verb: to link, to join, to connect Adverb: even
污染	wū rǎn	Noun: pollution, contamination Verb: to pollute, to contaminate
鼓励	gǔ lì	Verb: to encourage, to urge
降低	jiàng dī	Verb: to reduce, to lower
收入	shōu rù	Noun: income, revenue Verb: to take in
奖金	jiǎng jīn	Noun: premium, award money, bonus
收拾	shōu shi	Verb: to put in order, to tidy up, to punish
将来	jiāng lái	Noun: future Adverb: in the future
地址	dì zhǐ	Noun: address
降落	jiàng luò	Verb: to descend, to land
联系	lián xì	Noun: contact, connection Verb: to contact
应聘	yìng pìn	Verb: to apply for a job
其中	qí zhōng	Adverb: among, in
首先	shǒu xiān	Adverb: first of all
擦	cā	Verb: to wipe, to rub, to erase
故意	gù yì	Adverb: on purpose, deliberately
自然	zì rán	Noun: nature Adjective: natural
西红柿	xī hóng shì	Noun: tomato
挂	guà	Verb: to hang (up)
输	shū	Verb: to transport, to lose, to be beaten
猜	cāi	Verb: to guess
交	jiāo	Verb: to hand over, to intersect, to associate with
凉快	liáng kuai	Adjective: pleasantly cool
仔细	zǐ xì	Adjective: careful, attentive, cautious
自信	zì xìn	Noun: (self-)confidence Adjective: (self-)confident

骄傲	jiāo ào	Verb: to be proud of sth. Adjective: arrogant, conceited
勇敢	yǒng gǎn	Adjective: brave, courageous
掉	diào	Verb: to fall, to drop, to lose, to turn
千万	qiān wàn	Number: 10 million Adjective: countless, many Adverb: must, be sure to
材料	cái liào	Noun: material, data, stuff
调查	diào chá	Noun: investigation, survey Verb: to investigate, to survey
签证	qiān zhèng	Noun: visa
数量	shù liàng	Noun: amount, quantity
永远	yǒng yuǎn	Adverb: forever, ever
参观	cān guān	Verb: to visit, to look around
吸引	xī yǐn	Verb: to attract (interest, customers, etc.)
由	yóu	Relative Clause: due to, because of, by, from
丢	diū	Verb: to lose, to throw
交流	jiāo liú	Noun: communication, exchange Verb: to exchange, to communicate
郊区	jiāo qū	Noun: suburbs
关键	guān jiàn	Noun: key, crucial point
熟悉	shú xī	Verb: to be familiar with
优点	yōu diǎn	Noun: merit, advantage, strong point
总结	zǒng jié	Noun: summary Verb: to sum up
餐厅	cān tīng	Noun: restaurant
教授	jiào shòu	Noun: professor Verb: to instruct, to lecture on
零钱	líng qián	Noun: change (money)
管理	guǎn lǐ	Noun: management Verb: to manage
桥	qiáo	Noun: bridge
友好	yǒu hǎo	Adjective: friendly
交通	jiāo tōng	Noun: traffic

另外	lìng wài	Conjunction: in addition, moreover, furthermore
数字	shù zì	Noun: figure, number
停	tíng	Verb: to stop
敲	qiāo	Verb: to knock
教育	jiào yù	Noun: education Verb: to teach
留	liú	Verb: to keep, to remain, to stay, to leave (a message, etc.)
巧克力	qiǎo kè lì	Noun: chocolate
咸	xián	Adjective: salty
邮局	yóu jú	Noun: post office
饺子	jiǎo zi	Noun: dumpling
帅	shuài	Adjective: handsome, smart (for men)
厕所	cè suǒ	Noun: toilet
动作	dòng zuò	Noun: movement
节	jié	Noun: festival, holiday, segment, joint, part Verb: to save, to economize Measure Word: for segments
租	zū	Verb: to rent, to hire
观众	guān zhòng	Noun: audience, spectators
逛	guàng	Verb: to stroll
流利	liú lì	Adjective: fluent
现金	xiàn jīn	Noun: cash
幽默	yōu mò	Noun: humour Adjective: humorous
光	guāng	Noun: light, ray Adjective: naked Adverb: only, merely
流行	liú xíng	Verb: to spread Adjective: popular, fashionable
羡慕	xiàn mù	Verb: to envy, to admire
尤其	yóu qí	Adverb: especially, particularly
堵车	dǔ chē	Noun: traffic jam

广播	guǎng bō	Noun: broadcasting Verb: to broadcast
有趣	yǒu qù	Adjective: interesting
亲戚	qīn qi	Noun: relatives
差不多	chà bu duō	Adjective: almost, more or less
优秀	yōu xiù	Adjective: outstanding, excellent
肚子	dù zi	Noun: belly, abdomen
广告	guǎng gào	Noun: advertisement Verb: to advertise
顺便	shùn biàn	Adverb: on the way, in passing by
友谊	yǒu yì	Noun: friendship
结果	jié guǒ	Noun: result, outcome Conjunction: finally, at last
顺利	shùn lì	Adjective: smoothly
轻	qīng	Adjective: light, small in number, unimportant
顺序	shùn xù	Noun: sequence, order
由于	yóu yú	Relative Clause: due to, because of
转	zhuǎn	Verb: to turn, to change direction, to forward
最好	zuì hǎo	Adverb: it would be best, had better
尝	cháng	Verb: to taste Adverb: once
短信	duǎn xìn	Noun: text message
律师	lǜ shī	Noun: lawyer
场	chǎng	Noun: field, place Measure Word: for events, happenings, etc.
说明	shuō míng	Noun: explanation, illustration Verb: to explain, to illustrate
与	yǔ	Conjunction: and, with
长城	Cháng chéng	Noun: the Great Wall
规定	guī dìng	Noun: regulations, provision Verb: to fix, to stipulate
硕士	shuò shì	Noun: master's degree

响	xiǎng	Noun: sound, noise Verb: to make a sound Adjective: loud, noisy
香	xiāng	Adjective: fragrant
尊重	zūn zhòng	Noun: respect, esteem Verb: to respect, to honour
地点	dì diǎn	Noun: place, location
长江	Cháng jiāng	Noun: Yangtze river
乱	luàn	Noun: disorder Verb: to cause disorder Adjective: in a mess, confused
死	sǐ	Noun: death Verb: to die Adjective: dead
修理	xiū lǐ	Verb: to repair, to fix
情况	qíng kuàng	Noun: circumstance, situation
语法	yǔ fǎ	Noun: grammar
座	zuò	Noun: seat Measure Word: for cities, buildings, mountains, etc.
相反	xiāng fǎn	Adjective: opposite, contrary
愉快	yú kuài	Adjective: happy, cheerful
对话	duì huà	Noun: dialog
解释	jiě shì	Noun: explanation Verb: to explain
对面	duì miàn	Location: opposite
轻松	qīng sōng	Adjective: relaxed, easy
羽毛球	yǔ máo qiú	Noun: badminton
接受	jiē shòu	Verb: to accept, to receive
超过	chāo guò	Verb: to surpass, to exceed
对于	duì yú	Pronoun: regarding, as far as sth. is concerned
过程	guò chéng	Noun: process, course
麻烦	má fan	Verb: to trouble sbd. Adjective: troublesome
穷	qióng	Adjective: poor

座位	zuò wèi	Noun: seat, place
研究	yán jiū	Noun: research Verb: to research, to look into
马虎	mǎ hu	Adjective: careless, negligent, casual
于是	yú shì	Conjunction: as a result, consequently
国籍	guó jí	Noun: nationality, citizenship
节约	jié yuē	Verb: to economize, to conserve
橡皮	xiàng pí	Noun: rubber, eraser
预习	yù xí	Verb: to prepare for (a lesson)
国际	guó jì	Adjective: international
速度	sù dù	Noun: speed
语言	yǔ yán	Noun: language
接着	jiē zhe	Verb: to follow, to carry on Adverb: then, after that
取	qǔ	Verb: to take, to get
塑料袋	sù liào dài	Noun: plastic bag
作者	zuò zhě	Noun: author, writer
区别	qū bié	Noun: difference Verb: to distinguish
酸	suān	Adjective: sour
详细	xiáng xì	Adjective: detailed
满	mǎn	Verb: to fill, to satisfy Adjective: full, satisfied
随便	suí biàn	Adjective: random Adverb: as one wishes
原来	yuán lái	Adjective: former, original Adverb: as it turns out
尽管	jǐn guǎn	Adverb: unhesitatingly Conjunction: in spite of, although, despite
原谅	yuán liàng	Verb: to excuse, to forgive
而	ér	Conjunction: and, but, yet
毛	máo	Noun: hair, down Measure Word: for 0.1 RMB
全部	quán bù	Adjective: whole, entire, complete

随着	suí zhe	Relative Clause: along with, in the wake of
小吃	xiǎo chī	Noun: snack, refreshments
成功	chéng gōng	Noun: success Verb: to succeed
孙子	sūn zi	Noun: grandson
效果	xiào guǒ	Noun: effect, result
原因	yuán yīn	Noun: reason, cause
笑话	xiào hua	Noun: joke
儿童	ér tóng	Noun: child
毛巾	máo jīn	Noun: towel
却	què	Conjunction: but, yet
空	kòng	Noun: leisure, free time Verb: to leave empty, to empty
害羞	hài xiū	Adjective: shy
缺点	quē diǎn	Noun: weakness, shortcoming
小伙子	xiǎo huǒ zi	Noun: young fellow
海洋	hǎi yáng	Noun: ocean
进行	jìn xíng	Verb: to be in progress, be underway
阅读	yuè dú	Noun: reading Verb: to read
紧张	jǐn zhāng	Adjective: nervous, tense, in short supply
约会	yuē huì	Noun: appointment, engagement, date
汗	hàn	Noun: sweat
禁止	jìn zhǐ	Verb: to prohibit, to forbid, to ban
诚实	chéng shí	Adjective: honest, truthful
缺少	quē shǎo	Noun: lack, shortage Verb: to lack, to be short of
所有	suǒ yǒu	Verb: to possess, to own Adjective: all
生意	shēng yi	Noun: business, commerce
寒假	hán jià	Noun: winter vacation
精彩	jīng cǎi	Adjective: brilliant, excellent, splendid

确实	què shí	Adjective: indeed, really Adverb: for sure, indeed
警察	jǐng chá	Noun: police
航班	háng bān	Noun: scheduled flight, flight number
美丽	měi lì	Adjective: beautiful
成为	chéng wéi	Verb: to become, to turn into
法律	fǎ lǜ	Noun: law
然而	rán ér	Conjunction: however, but
台	tái	Noun: desk, platform Measure Word: for vehicles, machines, etc.
允许	yǔn xǔ	Verb: to permit, to allow
经济	jīng jì	Noun: economy
抬	tái	Verb: to lift up, to raise, to carry
小说	xiǎo shuō	Noun: novel, fiction
京剧	jīng jù	Noun: Beijing Opera
杂志	zá zhì	Noun: magazine
发生	fā shēng	Verb: to happen, to occur, to take place
好处	hǎo chu	Noun: benefit, advantage
经历	jīng lì	Noun: experience Verb: to experience
态度	tài du	Noun: manner, attitude
消息	xiāo xi	Noun: news, information
乘坐	chéng zuò	Verb: to ride (in a vehicle)
梦	mèng	Noun: dream
号码	hào mǎ	Noun: number
竟然	jìng rán	Adverb: unexpectedly
发展	fā zhǎn	Noun: development, growth Verb: to develop, to grow
好像	hǎo xiàng	Verb: to seem, to be like, look like
景色	jǐng sè	Noun: scenery, view, landscape
吃惊	chī jīng	Verb: to be startled, to be shocked, to be amazed

迷路	mí lù	Verb: to get lost, to lose the way
热闹	rè nao	Adjective: lively, busy
谈	tán	Verb: to talk
反对	fǎn duì	Verb: to fight against, to oppose
经验	jīng yàn	Noun: experience Verb: to experience
密码	mì mǎ	Noun: password
弹钢琴	tán gāng qín	Verb: to play the piano
咱们	zán men	Pronoun: we, us
竞争	jìng zhēng	Noun: competition Verb: to compete
暂时	zàn shí	Adjective: temporary
镜子	jìng zi	Noun: mirror
脏	zāng	Adjective: dirty
烦恼	fán nǎo	Noun: worries Adjective: worried, troubled
合格	hé gé	Adjective: qualified
趟	tàng	Measure Word: for number of trips or runs made
任何	rèn hé	Adjective: any, whichever, whatever
互联网	hù lián wǎng	Noun: internet
躺	tǎng	Verb: to lie (down), to recline
信封	xìn fēng	Noun: envelope
免费	miǎn fèi	Adjective: free (of charge)
汤	tāng	Noun: soup
照	zhào	Verb: to shine, to illuminate, to take (a photo) Relative Clause: according to
翻译	fān yì	Noun: translation, translator Verb: to translate
合适	hé shì	Adjective: suitable, appropriate
辛苦	xīn kǔ	Adjective: hard, toilsome
责任	zé rèn	Noun: duty, responsibility
重新	chóng xīn	Adverb: again

心情	xīn qíng	Noun: mood, state of mind
究竟	jiū jìng	Adverb: after all, actually
盒子	hé zi	Noun: box, case
秒	miǎo	Time: second
讨论	tǎo lùn	Noun: discussion Verb: to discuss
增加	zēng jiā	Verb: to increase, to raise
举	jǔ	Verb: to raise, to hold up, to elect
讨厌	tǎo yàn	Verb: to hate Adjective: disgusting, nasty
举办	jǔ bàn	Verb: to hold, to conduct
任务	rèn wu	Noun: mission, task
信息	xìn xī	Noun: information, news
抽烟	chōu yān	Verb: to smoke (a cigarette, etc.)
特点	tè diǎn	Noun: characteristic feature
民族	mín zú	Noun: nationality, ethnic group
信心	xìn xīn	Noun: confidence, faith
房东	fáng dōng	Noun: landlord
聚会	jù huì	Noun: party, gathering Verb: to party, to get together
扔	rēng	Verb: to throw (away)
方法	fāng fǎ	Noun: method, way
拒绝	jù jué	Verb: to refuse, to decline
仍然	réng rán	Adverb: still, yet
出差	chū chāi	Verb: to go on a business trip
行	xíng	Verb: to walk, to go Adjective: capable, competent Expression: OK
出发	chū fā	Verb: to leave, to set out
厚	hòu	Adjective: thick, deep
距离	jù lí	Noun: distance Verb: to be apart from

占线	zhàn xiàn	Adjective: busy (phone)
方面	fāng miàn	Noun: aspect, respect
醒	xǐng	Verb: to wake up
放弃	fàng qì	Verb: to give up
后悔	hòu huǐ	Verb: to regret, to repent
日记	rì jì	Noun: diary
提	tí	Verb: to carry, to raise
性别	xìng bié	Noun: gender, sex
放暑假	fàng shǔ jià	Verb: to take summer vacation
放松	fàng sōng	Verb: to relax, to loosen
兴奋	xīng fèn	Noun: excitement Adjective: excited
提供	tí gōng	Verb: to offer, to supply, to provide
幸福	xìng fú	Noun: happiness Adjective: happy
方向	fāng xiàng	Noun: direction, orientation
性格	xìng gé	Noun: nature, temperament, character
出现	chū xiàn	Verb: to appear, to arise
表示	biǎo shì	Verb: to express, to show, to indicate
厨房	chú fáng	Noun: kitchen
果汁	guǒ zhī	Noun: fruit juice
葡萄	pú tao	Noun: grape
糖	táng	Noun: sugar, sweets, candy
词语	cí yǔ	Noun: word, expression
普通话	pǔ tōng huà	Noun: Mandarin
低	dī	Adjective: low
眼镜	yǎn jìng	Noun: eyeglasses
表演	biǎo yǎn	Noun: performance, show Verb: to perform, to act
敢	gǎn	Auxiliary Verb: to dare

使	shǐ	Noun: envoy, messenger Verb: to make, to cause, to use, to employ
举行	jǔ xíng	Verb: to hold (meeting, etc.)
作用	zuò yòng	Noun: action, function, impact, effect Verb: to affect
以为	yǐ wéi	Verb: to think (wrongly), to be under the (wrong) impression
云	yún	Noun: cloud
相同	xiāng tóng	Adjective: identical, same

HSK 5

忽然	hū rán	Adverb: suddenly
捐	juān	Noun: tax, contribution Verb: to contribute, to donate, to give up
幸亏	xìng kuī	Adverb: fortunately, luckily
分手	fēn shǒu	Verb: to break up
除夕	chú xī	Noun: New Year's Eve
摸	mō	Verb: to touch, to feel with the hand, to grope
题目	tí mù	Noun: topic, title
照常	zhào cháng	Adverb: as usual
出席	chū xí	Verb: to attend, to be present
非	fēi	Adjective: wrong, mistaken Adverb: not, non-, un-
忽视	hū shì	Verb: to neglect, to ignore, to overlook
模仿	mó fǎng	Verb: to imitate, to copy
招待	zhāo dài	Noun: reception Verb: to entertain (guests), to serve, to receive
胡说	hú shuō	Verb: to talk nonsense
绝对	jué duì	Adjective: absolute, unconditional
模糊	mó hu	Adjective: fuzzy, blurred, indistinct
如何	rú hé	Adverb: how, in what way
体贴	tǐ tiē	Adjective: considerate
文字	wén zì	Noun: character
废话	fèi huà	Expression: nonsense, useless statement
胡同	hú tòng	Noun: lane, alley
决赛	jué sài	Noun: final (competition)
陌生	mò shēng	Adjective: strange, unfamiliar
如今	rú jīn	Time: nowadays
提问	tí wèn	Verb: to raise a question
行人	xíng rén	Noun: pedestrian

报到	bào dào	Verb: to check in, to register, to report for duty
唉	āi	Particle: uh (sigh)
糊涂	hú tu	Adjective: confused, muddled
角色	jué sè	Noun: character (in a book, play, etc.)
摩托车	mó tuō chē	Noun: motorbike
体现	tǐ xiàn	Verb: to embody, to incarnate
形容	xíng róng	Noun: description Verb: to describe
召开	zhào kāi	Verb: to convene, to convoke, to call together
网络	wǎng luò	Noun: network, internet
呼吸	hū xī	Verb: to breathe
决心	jué xīn	Noun: determination, resolution Verb: to make up one's mind
某	mǒu	Pronoun: some, certain
软	ruǎn	Adjective: soft
形势	xíng shì	Noun: situation, circumstances, terrain
着凉	zháo liáng	Verb: to catch a cold
爱护	ài hù	Verb: to cherish, to take good care of
传播	chuán bō	Verb: to spread, to propagate, to disseminate
肥皂	féi zào	Noun: soap
军事	jūn shì	Noun: military affairs
目标	mù biāo	Noun: goal, target, objective
软件	ruǎn jiàn	Noun: software
体验	tǐ yàn	Verb: to experience (for oneself)
形式	xíng shì	Noun: form, shape
均匀	jūn yún	Adjective: even, homogeneous
弱	ruò	Adjective: weak
行为	xíng wéi	Noun: action, conduct, behaviour, activity
培训	péi xùn	Noun: training Verb: to train, to cultivate
爱惜	ài xī	Verb: to cherish, to treasure

传染	chuán rǎn	Verb: to infect, to be contagious
卡车	kǎ chē	Noun: truck, lorry
目录	mù lù	Noun: catalogue, table of contents
洒	sǎ	Verb: to sprinkle, to spray
形象	xíng xiàng	Noun: image, appearance, figure
爱心	ài xīn	Noun: tender feelings, affections
传说	chuán shuō	Noun: legend, folklore Verb: it is said, that...
分别	fēn bié	Noun: difference Verb: to leave each other, to distinguish Adverb: separate
目前	mù qián	Time: at present, now
幸运	xìng yùn	Noun: luck, fortune Adjective: lucky, fortunate
暗	àn	Adjective: dark
传统	chuán tǒng	Noun: tradition Adjective: traditional
分布	fēn bù	Verb: to distribute, to be distributed
性质	xìng zhì	Noun: nature, character
报社	bào shè	Noun: newspaper office
岸	àn	Noun: shore, beach, coast
奋斗	fèn dòu	Verb: to fight for, to strive for
开发	kāi fā	Verb: to develop (e.g. IT), to exploit (a resource)
木头	mù tou	Noun: log of wood, blockhead
天空	tiān kōng	Noun: sky
形状	xíng zhuàng	Noun: form, shape
哲学	zhé xué	Noun: philosophy
闯	chuǎng	Verb: to rush, to break through, to charge
纷纷	fēn fēn	Adverb: one after another
开放	kāi fàng	Verb: to open up (for public, etc.)
嗓子	sǎng zi	Noun: throat, voice

胸	xiōng	Noun: chest
阵	zhèn	Noun: disposition of troops Measure Word: for short periods or events
抱怨	bào yuàn	Verb: to complain, to grumble
花生	huā shēng	Noun: peanut
开幕式	kāi mù shì	Noun: opening ceremony
兄弟	xiōng dì	Noun: brothers
窗帘	chuāng lián	Noun: window curtains
分配	fēn pèi	Verb: to assign, to allocate
话题	huà tí	Noun: topic
傻	shǎ	Adjective: foolish
天真	tiān zhēn	Adjective: naive, innocent
振动	zhèn dòng	Noun: vibration Verb: to vibrate
创造	chuàng zào	Noun: creation Verb: to create, to produce
分析	fēn xī	Noun: analysis Verb: to analyse
化学	huà xué	Noun: chemistry
哪怕	nǎ pà	Conjunction: even if
杀	shā	Verb: to kill
诊断	zhěn duàn	Noun: diagnosis Verb: to diagnose
香肠	xiāng cháng	Noun: sausage
安慰	ān wèi	Noun: comfort, consolation Verb: to comfort, to console
吹	chuī	Verb: to blow, to boast, to fail
华裔	huá yì	Noun: ethnic Chinese (but non-Chinese citizen)
针对	zhēn duì	Verb: to be aimed at, to be directed against
沙漠	shā mò	Noun: desert
调皮	tiáo pí	Adjective: naughty, tricky
修改	xiū gǎi	Noun: modification Verb: to modify, to amend, to revise

安装	ān zhuāng	Noun: installation Verb: to install, to mount
讽刺	fěng cì	Noun: irony, sarcasm Verb: to mock
砍	kǎn	Verb: to chop, to cut down
沙滩	shā tān	Noun: beach
真实	zhēn shí	Adjective: real, true
怀念	huái niàn	Verb: to cherish the memory of, to think of
看不起	kàn bu qǐ	Verb: to look down upon
晒	shài	Verb: to share files, to dry in the sun, to sunbathe
挑战	tiǎo zhàn	Noun: challenge
休闲	xiū xián	Noun: leisure
风格	fēng gé	Noun: style
删除	shān chú	Verb: to delete
调整	tiáo zhěng	Noun: adjustment Verb: to adjust, to revise
珍惜	zhēn xī	Verb: to value, to cherish
刺激	cì jī	Noun: stimulus, provocation Verb: to provoke, to stimulate, to excite
风景	fēng jǐng	Noun: scenery, landscape
难怪	nán guài	Expression: no wonder (that)
闪电	shǎn diàn	Noun: lightning
叙述	xù shù	Noun: narration Verb: to tell, to relate
或许	huò xǔ	Adverb: perhaps, maybe
维修	wéi xiū	Noun: maintenance Verb: to maintain, to protect
平安	píng'ān	Noun: peace Adjective: peaceful
此外	cǐ wài	Conjunction: besides, moreover
疯狂	fēng kuáng	Noun: madness Adjective: crazy, mad
善良	shàn liáng	Adjective: kind-hearted, good, honest

虚心	xū xīn	Adjective: modest
正	zhèng	Adjective: upright, honest Adverb: just, upright
把握	bǎ wò	Noun: assurance Verb: to grasp, to hold
次要	cì yào	Adjective: secondary, subordinate
风俗	fēng sú	Noun: (social) custom
缓解	huǎn jiě	Verb: to ease, to blunt, to help relieve (a crisis)
善于	shàn yú	Verb: to be good at
睁	zhēng	Verb: to open (the eyes)
一律	yí lǜ	Adjective: same, uniformly Adverb: all, without exception
风险	fēng xiǎn	Noun: risk, venture
扇子	shàn zi	Noun: fan
宣布	xuān bù	Verb: to declare, to announce
词汇	cí huì	Noun: vocabulary, words and phrases
辞职	cí zhí	Verb: to resign
否定	fǒu dìng	Noun: negation Verb: to negate, to deny
幻想	huàn xiǎng	Noun: illusion, fantasy Verb: to dream
通常	tōng cháng	Adverb: regular, usually, normally
宣传	xuān chuán	Noun: propaganda Verb: to propagate, to disseminate
胃口	wèi kǒu	Noun: appetite
摆	bǎi	Noun: pendulum Verb: to put, to place, to arrange
否认	fǒu rèn	Verb: to deny
脑袋	nǎo dai	Noun: head, skull, brain
政府	zhèng fǔ	Noun: government
从此	cóng cǐ	Conjunction: from now on
上当	shàng dàng	Verb: to be fooled
痛苦	tòng kǔ	Noun: pain, suffering Adjective: painful

整个	zhěng gè	Adjective: whole, entire
从而	cóng ér	Conjunction: thus, thereby
幅	fú	Measure Word: for pictures, paintings, textiles, etc.
痛快	tòng kuài	Adjective: delighted, very happy
血	xuè	Noun: blood
扶	fú	Verb: to help (sbd. up)
克	kè	Verb: to subdue, to restrain Measure Word: 1 gram
内科	nèi kē	Noun: internal medicine
证件	zhèng jiàn	Noun: certificate
位于	wèi yú	Verb: to lie, to be located at
匆忙	cōng máng	Adjective: hasty, hurried
商品	shāng pǐn	Noun: good, commodity
证据	zhèng jù	Noun: evidence, proof
一再	yí zài	Adverb: repeatedly, again and again
黄金	huáng jīn	Noun: gold
嫩	nèn	Adjective: tender, soft, inexperienced
办理	bàn lǐ	Verb: to handle, to conduct
从前	cóng qián	Time: previously, formerly
辅导	fǔ dǎo	Noun: coaching Verb: to tutor, to coach
慌张	huāng zhāng	Adjective: confused, flustered
颗	kē	Measure Word: for grain, pearls, teeth, stars, etc.
学术	xué shù	Noun: learning, science
争论	zhēng lùn	Noun: argument, debate Verb: to argue, to debate
从事	cóng shì	Verb: to engage in, to do (formal)
能干	néng gàn	Adjective: able, capable, competent
学问	xué wen	Noun: knowledge
醋	cù	Noun: vinegar

课程	kè chéng	Noun: course, class
商业	shāng yè	Noun: business, commerce, trade
整齐	zhěng qí	Adjective: neat, tidy, in good order
昆虫	kūn chóng	Noun: insect
促进	cù jìn	Verb: to promote, to advance
挥	huī	Verb: to wave, to brandish, to wipe away
克服	kè fú	Verb: to overcome, to conquer, to put up with
能源	néng yuán	Noun: energy, energy source
统一	tǒng yī	Verb: to unify, to unite, to integrate
傍晚	bàng wǎn	Time: towards evening, at nightfall
促使	cù shǐ	Verb: to urge, to push, to promote
妇女	fù nǚ	Noun: woman
灰	huī	Noun: ash, dust Adjective: grey
客观	kè guān	Adjective: objective, impartial
训练	xùn liàn	Noun: training Verb: to train, to drill
征求	zhēng qiú	Verb: to solicit, to seek, to ask for
灰尘	huī chén	Noun: dust
可见	kě jiàn	Conjunction: it is obvious that, it can clearly be seen that
迅速	xùn sù	Adjective: rapid, speedy, quick
争取	zhēng qǔ	Verb: to strive for, to fight for
薄	báo	Adjective: thin
催	cuī	Verb: to urge, to press
可靠	kě kào	Adjective: reliable, dependable
念	niàn	Verb: to read aloud
蛇	shé	Noun: snake
询问	xún wèn	Verb: to inquire
时差	shí chā	Noun: time difference
恢复	huī fù	Verb: to recover, to restore

刻苦	kè kǔ	Adjective: hardworking, assiduous
年代	nián dài	Time: decade, age, period
设备	shè bèi	Noun: equipment, facilities
透明	tòu míng	Adjective: transparent
寻找	xún zhǎo	Verb: to seek, to look for
存在	cún zài	Verb: to exist
汇率	huì lǜ	Noun: exchange rate
舍不得	shě bu de	Verb: reluctant to give up or let go
投资	tóu zī	Noun: investment Verb: to invest
整体	zhěng tǐ	Noun: whole entity
灰心	huī xīn	Verb: to lose heart, to be discouraged
年纪	nián jì	Noun: age
吐	tù	Verb: to vomit
宝贝	bǎo bèi	Noun: darling, baby
措施	cuò shī	Noun: measure, step
可怕	kě pà	Adjective: awful, terrible
设计	shè jì	Noun: design, plan Verb: to design, to plan
突出	tū chū	Adjective: outstanding
政治	zhèng zhì	Noun: politics
保持	bǎo chí	Verb: to keep, to maintain, to preserve
复制	fù zhì	Verb: to copy, to reproduce
射击	shè jī	Verb: to shoot, to fire (a gun)
土地	tǔ dì	Noun: land, soil, territory
直	zhí	Verb: to straighten Adjective: straight, direct
保存	bǎo cún	Verb: to conserve, to keep, to save (IT)
服装	fú zhuāng	Noun: clothing, dress
婚礼	hūn lǐ	Noun: wedding
设施	shè shī	Noun: facility, installation

土豆	tǔ dòu	Noun: potato
靠	kào	Verb: to lean against, to get near
报道	bào dào	Noun: report Verb: to report
盖	gài	Noun: cover Verb: to cover
婚姻	hūn yīn	Noun: wedding, marriage
延长	yán cháng	Verb: to prolong, to extend
报告	bào gào	Noun: report, speech, talk Verb: to report
宁可	nìng kě	Conjunction: would rather, preferably
摄影	shè yǐng	Verb: to take a photo, to shoot a movie
朗读	lǎng dú	Verb: to read aloud
宝贵	bǎo guì	Adjective: valuable, precious
达到	dá dào	Verb: to achieve, to reach, to attain
改革	gǎi gé	Noun: reform Verb: to reform
伙伴	huǒ bàn	Noun: partner, companion, mate
兔子	tù zi	Noun: rabbit
包裹	bāo guǒ	Noun: parcel, package Verb: to wrap up
改进	gǎi jìn	Noun: improvement Verb: to improve
火柴	huǒ chái	Noun: match (for fire)
牛仔裤	niú zǎi kù	Noun: jeans
团	tuán	Noun: group, regiment Measure Word: for ball-like things
宴会	yàn huì	Noun: banquet, feast
支	zhī	Noun: branch, division Verb: to support Measure Word: for stick-like objects
包含	bāo hán	Verb: to contain, to embody, to include
大方	dà fang	Adjective: generous, of good taste
概括	gài kuò	Noun: summary Verb: to summarize; to generalize

浓	nóng	Adjective: dense, concentrated, thick
伸	shēn	Verb: to stretch, to extend
退	tuì	Verb: to return, to decline, to withdraw
概念	gài niàn	Noun: concept, idea
身材	shēn cái	Noun: figure, stature
指导	zhǐ dǎo	Noun: guidance Verb: to guide, to direct
包括	bāo kuò	Verb: to include, to consist of
打工	dǎ gōng	Noun: a part time job Verb: to work (temporary or casual)
改善	gǎi shàn	Noun: improvement Verb: to improve
农村	nóng cūn	Noun: village, rural area
身份	shēn fèn	Noun: identity, status
保留	bǎo liú	Noun: reservation Verb: to reserve, to hold back
改正	gǎi zhèng	Noun: correction Verb: to correct, to amend
空间	kōng jiān	Noun: space
农民	nóng mín	Noun: peasant, farmer
神话	shén huà	Noun: fairy tale, myth
退步	tuì bù	Noun: regression Verb: to regress, to fall behind, to go backward
打交道	dǎ jiāo dao	Verb: have dealings with
活跃	huó yuè	Adjective: active, vigorous
农业	nóng yè	Noun: agriculture, farming
严肃	yán sù	Adjective: solemn, serious
制定	zhì dìng	Verb: to formulate, to work out, to draw up
主题	zhǔ tí	Noun: topic, subject (e-mail)
深刻	shēn kè	Adjective: profound, deep
推辞	tuī cí	Verb: to decline, to turn down
制度	zhì dù	Noun: system

占	zhàn	Verb: to take possession of, to occupy
保险	bǎo xiǎn	Noun: insurance Verb: to insure Adjective: safe, secure
打喷嚏	dǎ pēn tì	Verb: to sneeze
推广	tuī guǎng	Verb: to spread, to popularize
冷淡	lěng dàn	Adjective: indifferent, cold, unconcerned
干脆	gān cuì	Adjective: clear-cut, straightforward Adverb: simply, you might as well
空闲	kòng xián	Noun: leisure Adjective: idle
神秘	shén mì	Noun: mystery Adjective: mysterious
推荐	tuī jiàn	Noun: recommendation Verb: to recommend
痒	yǎng	Verb: to itch, to tickle
智慧	zhì huì	Noun: wisdom, intelligence, knowledge
挣	zhèng	Verb: to earn, to make money
控制	kòng zhì	Noun: control Verb: to control
女士	nǚ shì	Noun: lady, madam
退休	tuì xiū	Noun: retirement Verb: to retire
指挥	zhǐ huī	Noun: conductor Verb: to conduct, to command, to direct
大厦	dà shà	Noun: large building, mansion
干活儿	gàn huó r	Verb: to work (often hard, manual work)
基本	jī běn	Adjective: basic, fundamental
感激	gǎn jī	Verb: to feel grateful, to be thankful
口味	kǒu wèi	Noun: taste, flavour
至今	zhì jīn	Time: until now, until today
打听	dǎ ting	Verb: to ask about, to inquire about, to nose into
赶紧	gǎn jǐn	Adverb: at once, losing no time
偶然	ǒu rán	Adverb: accidentally, by chance

样式	yàng shì	Noun: type, style, pattern
背	bèi	Noun: back Verb: to learn by heart
大象	dà xiàng	Noun: elephant
歪	wāi	Adjective: crooked, devious
阳台	yáng tái	Noun: balcony
治疗	zhì liáo	Noun: medical treatment Verb: to treat, to cure
大型	dà xíng	Adjective: large-scale
派	pài	Noun: school, group, pi (?) Verb: to send, to assign
升	shēng	Verb: to promote, to raise Measure Word: 1 litre
外交	wài jiāo	Noun: diplomacy, foreign affairs
支票	zhī piào	Noun: check (bank)
勿	wù	Adverb: (do) not
悲观	bēi guān	Adjective: pessimistic
赶快	gǎn kuài	Adverb: at once, immediately
夸	kuā	Verb: to praise, to boast
拍	pāi	Verb: to clap, to slap, to take (a photo)
摇	yáo	Verb: to shake, to sway
背景	bèi jǐng	Noun: background, context
答应	dā ying	Verb: to agree, to promise, to respond
及格	jí gé	Verb: to pass a test
生产	shēng chǎn	Noun: production Verb: to produce, to manufacture
集合	jí hé	Noun: congregation Verb: to gather, to assemble
声调	shēng diào	Noun: tone, note
被子	bèi zi	Noun: quilt
感受	gǎn shòu	Noun: feeling, perception Verb: to sense, to feel
会计	kuài jì	Noun: accountant, accounting

生动	shēng dòng	Adjective: vivid, lively
咬	yǎo	Verb: to bite
印刷	yìn shuā	Noun: printing Verb: to print
感想	gǎn xiǎng	Noun: impressions, reflections
腰	yāo	Noun: waist, lower back
秩序	zhì xù	Noun: order, orderly state
盼望	pàn wàng	Verb: to hope for, to look forward to
胜利	shèng lì	Noun: victory, triumph
要不	yào bù	Conjunction: otherwise
干燥	gān zào	Adjective: dry
宽	kuān	Adjective: wide, broad
省略	shěng lüè	Verb: to leave out, to omit
玩具	wán jù	Noun: toy
本科	běn kē	Noun: Bachelor course
完美	wán měi	Adjective: perfect
至于	zhì yú	Conjunction: to go so far as to, with regard to
呆	dāi	Verb: to stay Adjective: dull, foolish, stupid
志愿者	zhì yuàn zhě	Noun: volunteer
本领	běn lǐng	Noun: skill, ability, capability
代表	dài biǎo	Noun: representative Verb: to represent
钢铁	gāng tiě	Noun: steel
激烈	jī liè	Adjective: intense, fierce
完善	wán shàn	Verb: to improve, to make perfect Adjective: perfect
制造	zhì zào	Verb: to make, to manufacture
吸取	xī qǔ	Verb: to absorb, to assimilate
本质	běn zhì	Noun: essence, nature
搞	gǎo	Verb: to do, to make

系领带	jì lǐng dài	Verb: to tie one's necktie
扩大	kuò dà	Verb: to expand, to enlarge
执照	zhí zhào	Noun: license
贷款	dài kuǎn	Noun: loan Verb: to provide a loan
纪录	jì lù	Noun: record
赔偿	péi cháng	Noun: compensation Verb: to compensate
绳子	shéng zi	Noun: string, rope, cord
万一	wàn yī	Noun: contingency Conjunction: in case
夜	yè	Noun: night
制作	zhì zuò	Verb: to make, to manufacture, to produce
彼此	bǐ cǐ	Pronoun: each other, one another
代替	dài tì	Noun: replacement Verb: to replace, to substitute Relative Clause: instead of
告别	gào bié	Verb: to leave, to say good-bye to
记录	jì lù	Noun: record
佩服	pèi fu	Verb: to admire
完整	wán zhěng	Adjective: complete, intact
待遇	dài yù	Noun: treatment, pay, salary
高档	gāo dàng	Adjective: top grade
纪律	jì lǜ	Noun: discipline
配合	pèi hé	Verb: to coordinate, to cooperate, to fit
淡	dàn	Adjective: mild, (rather) tasteless, light in colour
高级	gāo jí	Adjective: high level, high grade, advanced
急忙	jí máng	Adjective: hasty, in a hurry
辣椒	là jiāo	Noun: hot pepper, chili
培养	péi yǎng	Verb: to train, to cultivate, to bring up
往返	wǎng fǎn	Adverb: back and forth, to and from

业务	yè wù	Noun: business, professional work
假设	jiǎ shè	Noun: hypothesis, assumption Verb: to suppose, to assume Conjunction: in case of
毕竟	bì jìng	Adverb: after all, in the end
单纯	dān chún	Adjective: pure, simple
寂寞	jì mò	Adjective: lonely
盆	pén	Noun: basin, tub, pot Measure Word: for approx. 128 litres
比例	bǐ lì	Noun: proportion, scale
单调	dān diào	Adjective: monotonous, dull
纪念	jì niàn	Noun: commemoration Verb: to commemorate
诗	shī	Noun: poem
连续	lián xù	Adjective: in a row, consecutive
避免	bì miǎn	Verb: to avoid, to prevent
单独	dān dú	Adjective: alone, solo
极其	jí qí	Adverb: extremely
业余	yè yú	Noun: spare time Adjective: amateur
必然	bì rán	Adjective: inevitable, certain
机器	jī qì	Noun: machine
匹	pǐ	Noun: ordinary person Measure Word: for horses and cloth
士兵	shì bīng	Noun: soldier
中介	zhōng jiè	Noun: agency, agent
当心	dāng xīn	Verb: to take care, to watch out
担任	dān rèn	Verb: to hold the post of, to serve as
批	pī	Verb: to criticize Measure Word: for batches, lots, etc.
市场	shì chǎng	Noun: market
王子	wáng zǐ	Noun: prince
亿	yì	Number: 100 million

重量	zhòng liàng	Noun: weight
用功	yòng gōng	Adjective: diligent, hardworking
隔壁	gé bì	Location: next door
肌肉	jī ròu	Noun: muscle
披	pī	Verb: to drape over one's shoulder, to crack
时代	shí dài	Time: time, era, epoch
单位	dān wèi	Noun: unit
个别	gè bié	Adjective: exceptional, very few, individual
拦	lán	Verb: to block, to hinder
似的	shì de	Conjunction: (seems) as if
乙	yǐ	Number: second(ly)
耽误	dān wu	Verb: to delay
烂	làn	Verb: to rot Adjective: rotten, mushy, soft
种类	zhǒng lèi	Noun: kind, type, sort, variety
必要	bì yào	Adjective: necessary, essential
胆小鬼	dǎn xiǎo guǐ	Noun: coward
疲劳	pí láo	Noun: wariness, fatigue Adjective: tired, weary, exhausted
胃	wèi	Noun: stomach
中心	zhōng xīn	Noun: centre
计算	jì suàn	Noun: calculation Verb: to count, to calculate
尾巴	wěi ba	Noun: tail
一辈子	yí bèi zi	Noun: a lifetime
中旬	zhōng xún	Time: middle third of a month
播放	bō fàng	Verb: to broadcast, to transmit
单元	dān yuán	Noun: unit, cell, entrance number
个人	gè rén	Noun: individual Adjective: individual
集体	jí tǐ	Noun: collective

未必	wèi bì	Adverb: not necessarily
挡	dǎng	Verb: to block, to hinder, to obstruct
格外	gé wài	Adverb: especially, particularly
伟大	wěi dà	Adjective: great, mighty
一旦	yí dàn	Time: in one day Conjunction: in case, if, once
兼职	jiān zhí	Noun: part-time job Adjective: part-time
夏令营	xià lìng yíng	Noun: summer camp
便	biàn	Verb: to relieve oneself Adjective: convenient, handy Adverb: then, in that case
个性	gè xìng	Noun: personality, character
记忆	jì yì	Noun: memory Verb: to remember
批准	pī zhǔn	Verb: to approve, to ratify
实话	shí huà	Noun: truth
周到	zhōu dao	Adjective: thoughtful, considerate
老百姓	lǎo bǎi xìng	Noun: ordinary people
违反	wéi fǎn	Verb: to violate (law)
移动	yí dòng	Noun: movement Verb: to move, to shift Adjective: mobile, portable
岛屿	dǎo yǔ	Noun: islands
编辑	biān jí	Noun: editor, compiler Verb: to edit, to compile
当地	dāng dì	Noun: locality Adjective: local
集中	jí zhōng	Verb: to concentrate, to focus
老板	lǎo bǎn	Noun: boss, owner
片	piàn	Noun: thin piece, slice, film Measure Word: for movies, scenes, etc., pieces of things
危害	wēi hài	Noun: endangerment Verb: to endanger, to harm

辩论	biàn lùn	Noun: debate, argument Verb: to debate, to argue
各自	gè zì	Adverb: each, respective
嫁	jià	Verb: to marry (woman -> men)
劳动	láo dòng	Noun: work, labour
实践	shí jiàn	Verb: to practice, to carry out
数	shǔ	Verb: to count
鞭炮	biān pào	Noun: firecrackers
片面	piàn miàn	Adjective: unilateral, one-sided
围巾	wéi jīn	Noun: scarf
遗憾	yí hàn	Verb: to regret Adjective: regrettable
表达	biǎo dá	Verb: to express, to convey
甲	jiǎ	Number: first(ly)
劳驾	láo jià	Expression: excuse me
未来	wèi lái	Noun: future
煮	zhǔ	Verb: to cook, to boil
标点	biāo diǎn	Noun: punctuation, punctuation mark
根	gēn	Noun: root, origin Measure Word: for long, slender objects
姥姥	lǎo lao	Noun: grandmother (mother's mum)
使劲儿	shǐ jìn r	Verb: to exert all one's strength
猪	zhū	Noun: pig
轻易	qīng yì	Adverb: easily, lightly
根本	gēn běn	Noun: foundation, root Adjective: fundamental, simply, basic
老实	lǎo shi	Adjective: honest, sincere
飘	piāo	Verb: to flutter, to float (in the wind)
试卷	shì juàn	Noun: examination paper
委屈	wěi qu	Verb: to feel wronged
以及	yǐ jí	Conjunction: as well as

逐步	zhú bù	Adverb: step by step
表面	biǎo miàn	Noun: surface, outside, appearance
嘉宾	jiā bīn	Noun: honoured guest
时刻	shí kè	Time: moment
围绕	wéi rào	Verb: to revolve around, to surround
注册	zhù cè	Verb: to register
表明	biǎo míng	Verb: to show, to indicate, to make clear
老鼠	lǎo shǔ	Noun: rat, mouse
频道	pín dào	Noun: frequency, (TV) channel
时髦	shí máo	Adjective: fashionable
主持	zhǔ chí	Verb: to direct, to manage, to preside over
表情	biǎo qíng	Noun: expression
到达	dào dá	Verb: to arrive, to reach
失眠	shī mián	Noun: insomnia Verb: be unable to sleep
以来	yǐ lái	Adverb: since
主动	zhǔ dòng	Verb: to take the initiative Adjective: active
国王	guó wáng	Noun: king
道德	dào dé	Noun: morality, ethics
公布	gōng bù	Verb: to announce, to make public
假如	jiǎ rú	Conjunction: if
乐观	lè guān	Adjective: optimistic, hopeful
凭	píng	Noun: proof Verb: to rely on, to lean against Relative Clause: according to, on the basis of
祝福	zhù fú	Verb: to bless, to wish well
表现	biǎo xiàn	Verb: to show, to express, to display
工厂	gōng chǎng	Noun: factory
驾驶	jià shǐ	Verb: to drive, to pilot
雷	léi	Noun: thunder

平	píng	Adjective: flat, level, calm, peaceful
时期	shí qī	Noun: period, phase
议论	yì lùn	Noun: discussion Verb: to discuss, to comment on
道理	dào lǐ	Noun: principle, reason, argument
工程师	gōng chéng shī	Noun: engineer
家庭	jiā tíng	Noun: family, household
平常	píng cháng	Adjective: ordinary, common Adverb: generally, usually
微笑	wēi xiào	Noun: smile Verb: to smile
移民	yí mín	Noun: immigrant Verb: to immigrate, to migrate
主观	zhǔ guān	Adjective: subjective
乐器	yuè qì	Noun: musical instrument
倒霉	dǎo méi	Verb: to have bad luck
家务	jiā wù	Noun: housework
平等	píng děng	Noun: equality Adjective: equal
失去	shī qù	Verb: to lose (sth.)
威胁	wēi xié	Noun: threat, menace Verb: to threaten, to menace
字母	zì mǔ	Noun: letter (alphabet)
标志	biāo zhì	Noun: symbol, sign Verb: to symbolize, to indicate
家乡	jiā xiāng	Noun: hometown, native place
平方	píng fāng	Noun: square
湿润	shī rùn	Adjective: moist, humid
唯一	wéi yī	Adverb: only, sole
逐渐	zhú jiàn	Adverb: gradually
导演	dǎo yǎn	Noun: director (film, etc.) Verb: to direct
时尚	shí shàng	Noun: fashion
位置	wèi zhì	Noun: position, place

工具	gōng jù	Noun: tool, utensil
价值	jià zhí	Noun: value, worth
平衡	píng héng	Noun: balance, equilibrium
事实	shì shí	Noun: fact
闻	wén	Verb: to hear, to smell
依然	yī rán	Adverb: still, as before
主人	zhǔ rén	Noun: host, master
导致	dǎo zhì	Verb: to lead to, to create, to bring about
公开	gōng kāi	Verb: to publish, to make public Adjective: public
假装	jiǎ zhuāng	Verb: to pretend
梨	lí	Noun: pear
评价	píng jià	Verb: to assess, to evaluate
石头	shí tou	Noun: stone
主席	zhǔ xí	Noun: chairman
夹子	jiā zi	Noun: clip, clamp, tongs
平静	píng jìng	Noun: calm, quiet, tranquil
吻	wěn	Noun: kiss Verb: to kiss
功能	gōng néng	Noun: function, feature
平均	píng jūn	Noun: average Adjective: average, mean
食物	shí wù	Noun: food
稳定	wěn dìng	Noun: stability Verb: to stabilize Adjective: steady, stable
病毒	bìng dú	Noun: virus
公平	gōng píng	Adjective: fair, impartial
捡	jiǎn	Verb: to pick up, to gather
事物	shì wù	Noun: thing, object
意外	yì wài	Noun: accident Adjective: unexpected, accidental

工人	gōng rén	Noun: worker
实习	shí xí	Noun: practice, internship Verb: to practice
问候	wèn hòu	Verb: to send a greeting
主张	zhǔ zhāng	Noun: viewpoint, stand Verb: to advocate, to stand for
肩膀	jiān bǎng	Noun: shoulder
实现	shí xiàn	Verb: to realize, to achieve, to bring about
疑问	yí wèn	Noun: question, doubt
竹子	zhú zi	Noun: bamboo
事先	shì xiān	Adverb: in advance, beforehand
文件	wén jiàn	Noun: document, file
义务	yì wù	Noun: duty, obligation Adjective: voluntary
抓紧	zhuā jǐn	Verb: to grasp firmly, to pay special attention to, to seize
玻璃	bō li	Noun: glass
贡献	gòng xiàn	Noun: contribution Verb: to contribute, to dedicate
离婚	lí hūn	Noun: divorce Verb: to divorce (from)
破产	pò chǎn	Noun: bankruptcy Verb: to go bankrupt
文具	wén jù	Noun: stationery, writing materials
工业	gōng yè	Noun: industry
立即	lì jí	Adverb: immediately, at once
破坏	pò huài	Noun: destruction, damage Verb: to destroy, to break
实验	shí yàn	Noun: experiment Verb: to experiment
文明	wén míng	Noun: civilization, culture Adjective: civilized
意义	yì yì	Noun: meaning, sense, significance
转变	zhuǎn biàn	Noun: change Verb: to change, to transform
老婆	lǎo po	Noun: wife, female partner

博物馆	bó wù guǎn	Noun: museum
等待	děng dài	Verb: to wait for, to await
公寓	gōng yù	Noun: block of flats
剪刀	jiǎn dāo	Noun: scissors
迫切	pò qiè	Adjective: urgent, pressing
失业	shī yè	Noun: unemployment Verb: to lose one's job Adjective: unemployed
温暖	wēn nuǎn	Adjective: warm
转告	zhuǎn gào	Verb: to pass on (a message, etc.), to transmit
脖子	bó zi	Noun: neck
温柔	wēn róu	Adjective: gentle, soft, tender
一致	yí zhì	Noun: agreement Adjective: identical, unanimous (views, etc.)
专家	zhuān jiā	Noun: expert, specialist
组	zǔ	Noun: group, team Verb: to organize, to form
登记	dēng jì	Verb: to register
公元	gōng yuán	Noun: Christian era
艰巨	jiān jù	Adjective: arduous, formidable
立刻	lì kè	Adverb: immediately, at once
实用	shí yòng	Adjective: practical, pragmatic, applied
无所谓	wú suǒ wèi	Expression: expressing indifference
在于	zài yú	Conjunction: to depend on, to lie in
布	bù	Noun: cloth
公主	gōng zhǔ	Noun: princess
坚决	jiān jué	Adjective: resolute, determined
力量	lì liàng	Noun: power, force, strength
文学	wén xué	Noun: literature
专心	zhuān xīn	Noun: concentration Verb: to concentrate Adjective: concentrated, attentive

不安	bù ān	Adjective: disturbed, uneasy
等于	děng yú	Verb: to equal, to amount to
理论	lǐ lùn	Noun: theory
银	yín	Noun: silver Adjective: silver (colour)
项	xiàng	Noun: neck, point, item Measure Word: for tasks, events, etc.
递	dì	Verb: to pass, to hand over
艰苦	jiān kǔ	Adjective: difficult, hard
始终	shǐ zhōng	Adverb: from beginning to end
撞	zhuàng	Verb: to hit, to bump against, to collide, to run into
补充	bǔ chōng	Noun: supplement Verb: to supplement, to complement Adjective: additional, supplementary
建立	jiàn lì	Verb: to build, to establish
厘米	lí mǐ	Measure Word: centimetre
狮子	shī zi	Noun: lion
装	zhuāng	Noun: dress, clothing, costume Verb: to pretend, to install, to fix, to load, to pack
碰	pèng	Verb: to meet, to run into
简历	jiǎn lì	Noun: CV, resume
卧室	wò shì	Noun: bedroom
因而	yīn ér	Conjunction: thus, as a result
状况	zhuàng kuàng	Noun: condition, state, situation
搜索	sōu suǒ	Verb: to search, to look for sth.
滴	dī	Verb: to drip, to drop Measure Word: for a drop
构成	gòu chéng	Verb: to compose, to constitute, to configure (IT)
握手	wò shǒu	Verb: to shake hands
装饰	zhuāng shì	Noun: decoration Verb: to decorate

交往	jiāo wǎng	Noun: association, contact Verb: to associate, to contact
不得了	bù dé liǎo	Adjective: disastrous, terrible Adverb: extremely, terribly
地道	dì dao	Adjective: authentic, genuine, real
沟通	gōu tōng	Verb: to communicate
键盘	jiàn pán	Noun: keyboard
利润	lì rùn	Noun: profit
期待	qī dài	Noun: expectation Verb: to look forward to
状态	zhuàng tài	Noun: state, condition
不断	bú duàn	Adverb: continuous, unceasing
坚强	jiān qiáng	Adjective: strong
启发	qǐ fā	Noun: inspiration, enlightenment Verb: to inspire, to enlighten
雾	wù	Noun: fog
追求	zhuī qiú	Verb: to pursue, to seek after
滑	huá	Verb: to slide Adjective: slippery, smooth
类型	lèixíng	Noun: type, category
古代	gǔ dài	Time: ancient times
因素	yīn sù	Noun: element, factor
熬夜	áo yè	Verb: to stay up all night
地理	dì lǐ	Noun: geography
利息	lì xī	Noun: interest (on a loan)
气氛	qì fēn	Noun: atmosphere, mood
冰激凌	bīng jī líng	Noun: ice cream
古典	gǔ diǎn	Adjective: classical
建设	jiàn shè	Noun: construction Verb: to build, to construct
手工	shǒu gōng	Noun: handwork Adjective: manual
物理	wù lǐ	Noun: physics

消极	xiāo jí	Adjective: negative, passive, inactive
迟早	chí zǎo	Expression: sooner or later
地区	dì qū	Noun: region, district, area
固定	gù dìng	Verb: to fasten, to fix Adjective: fixed, set, regular
利益	lì yì	Noun: benefit
收获	shōu huò	Noun: result, gain, harvest Verb: to harvest
出示	chū shì	Verb: to show, to display, to present
不见得	bú jiàn dé	Adverb: not necessarily, not likely
的确	dí què	Adverb: really, indeed
姑姑	gū gu	Noun: aunt (paternal)
利用	lì yòng	Verb: to make use of, to utilize
奇迹	qí jì	Noun: miracle, wonder
粗糙	cū cāo	Adjective: rough
敌人	dí rén	Noun: enemy
简直	jiǎn zhí	Adverb: simply, totally
理由	lǐ yóu	Noun: reason, justification
期间	qī jiān	Noun: period of time, period
无奈	wú nài	Verb: to have no choice
硬	yìng	Adjective: hard, stiff, firm
紫	zǐ	Adjective: purple
恭喜	gōng xǐ	Expression: congratulations
地毯	dì tǎn	Noun: carpet
建筑	jiàn zhù	Noun: building, architecture Verb: to build, to construct
收据	shōu jù	Noun: receipt
自从	zì cóng	Adverb: ever since Relative Clause: since
随身	suí shēn	Verb: to take with one
后背	hòu bèi	Noun: back (body)

部门	bù mén	Noun: department, branch
寿命	shòu mìng	Noun: life span, life expectancy
应付	yìng fu	Verb: to deal with, to cope with
随手	suí shǒu	Adverb: conveniently, without extra trouble
急诊	jí zhěn	Noun: emergency
无数	wú shù	Adjective: countless, innumerable
自动	zì dòng	Adjective: automatic
健身	jiàn shēn	Verb: to work out, to exercise
不耐烦	bú nài fán	Noun: impatience Adjective: impatient
地位	dì wèi	Noun: position, status
姑娘	gū niang	Noun: girl, young woman, daughter
恋爱	liàn ài	Noun: love Verb: to be in love, to have an affair
受伤	shòu shāng	Verb: to get injured
武术	wǔ shù	Noun: martial arts
硬件	yìng jiàn	Noun: hardware
资格	zī gé	Noun: qualifications
戒	jiè	Verb: to quit (e.g. smoking)
不然	bù rán	Conjunction: otherwise
股票	gǔ piào	Noun: share, stock
讲究	jiǎng jiu	Verb: to pay attention to Adjective: exquisite, tasteful
联合	lián hé	Noun: alliance, union Verb: to unite, to join Adjective: combined, joint
企业	qǐ yè	Noun: enterprise, company
物质	wù zhì	Noun: matter, substance, material
迎接	yíng jiē	Verb: to greet, to welcome, to meet
自豪	zì háo	Adjective: proud
夸张	kuā zhāng	Adjective: exaggerated, excessive
不如	bù rú	Verb: not as good as

地震	dì zhèn	Noun: earthquake
连忙	lián máng	Adverb: promptly, at once
汽油	qì yóu	Noun: gas, gasoline
手术	shǒu shù	Noun: operation, surgery
屋子	wū zi	Noun: room, house
英俊	yīng jùn	Adjective: handsome and smart
写作	xiě zuò	Noun: writing Verb: to write, to compose
在乎	zài hu	Verb: to care about, to mind, to be determined by
内部	nèi bù	Noun: internal matters Adjective: internal, inside, non-public
模特	mó tè	Noun: model (fashion)
不要紧	bú yào jǐn	Expression: it doesn't matter, never mind
其余	qí yú	Pronoun: the rest, the others
手套	shǒu tào	Noun: gloves
系	xì	Noun: system, department
资金	zī jīn	Noun: funds, capital
拼音	pīn yīn	Noun: Pinyin
步骤	bù zhòu	Noun: step, move, measure
骨头	gǔ tou	Noun: bone, strong character
酱油	jiàng yóu	Noun: soy sauce
自觉	zì jué	Adjective: aware, conscious, on one's own initiative
签	qiān	Verb: to sign
不足	bù zú	Noun: shortcomings Adjective: insufficient, not enough
电池	diàn chí	Noun: battery, electric cell
鼓舞	gǔ wǔ	Noun: encouragement Verb: to inspire, to animate
讲座	jiǎng zuò	Noun: lecture
手续	shǒu xù	Noun: procedure, formality
英雄	yīng xióng	Noun: hero

资料	zī liào	Noun: material, data, resources, profile (IT)
日子	rì zi	Noun: day
伤害	shāng hài	Verb: to injure sbd., to harm
商务	shāng wù	Noun: commerce, business
手指	shǒu zhǐ	Noun: finger
营养	yíng yǎng	Noun: nutrition, nourishment
字幕	zì mù	Noun: caption, subtitle
列车	liè chē	Noun: train
摔倒	shuāi dǎo	Verb: to fall down
亮	liàng	Verb: to shine, to show, to reveal Adjective: bright, clear, shiny
欠	qiàn	Verb: to owe Adjective: deficient
营业	yíng yè	Verb: to do business, to trade
外公	wài gōng	Noun: maternal grandfather
电台	diàn tái	Noun: broadcasting station, radio station
鼓掌	gǔ zhǎng	Verb: to applaud
浅	qiǎn	Adjective: shallow, light
应用	yìng yòng	Noun: application Verb: to apply, to use
姿势	zī shì	Noun: gesture, posture, pose
员工	yuán gōng	Noun: employee, staff
踩	cǎi	Verb: to stamp on, to step, to press a pedal
良好	liáng hǎo	Adjective: good, favourable, fine
影子	yǐng zi	Noun: shadow
自私	zì sī	Adjective: selfish
着火	zháo huǒ	Verb: to ignite, to start burning
鼠标	shǔ biāo	Noun: mouse (IT)
细节	xì jié	Noun: detail, particulars
装修	zhuāng xiū	Verb: to renovate
财产	cái chǎn	Noun: property, possession

点心	diǎn xin	Noun: light refreshments, Dimsum (Cantonese)
挂号	guà hào	Verb: to register
浇	jiāo	Verb: to water, to pour, to sprinkle
粮食	liáng shi	Noun: food, cereals
蔬菜	shū cài	Noun: vegetables
戏剧	xì jù	Noun: drama, play, theatre
拥抱	yōng bào	Verb: to embrace, to hug
乖	guāi	Adjective: obedient, well-behaved, clever, good
了不起	liǎo bu qǐ	Adjective: amazing, extraordinary
吸收	xī shōu	Verb: to absorb, to soak up, to assimilate
采访	cǎi fǎng	Verb: to interview, to gather news
怪不得	guài bu de	Conjunction: no wonder, so that is why
教材	jiào cái	Noun: teaching material
前途	qián tú	Noun: prospect, future
书架	shū jià	Noun: bookshelf
拥挤	yōng jǐ	Verb: to squeeze, to press Adjective: crowded
咨询	zī xún	Noun: consultation Verb: to consult, to seek advice
彩虹	cǎi hóng	Noun: rainbow
拐弯	guǎi wān	Verb: to turn a corner, to change direction
角度	jiǎo dù	Noun: angle, point of view
数据	shù jù	Noun: data
系统	xì tǒng	Noun: system
勇气	yǒng qì	Noun: courage
自由	zì yóu	Noun: freedom, liberty Adjective: free
钓	diào	Verb: to fish
狡猾	jiǎo huá	Adjective: sly, cunning, tricky
谦虚	qiān xū	Adjective: modest

熟练	shú liàn	Adjective: skilled, practiced, proficient
用途	yòng tú	Noun: application, use, purpose
自愿	zì yuàn	Adjective: voluntary
采取	cǎi qǔ	Verb: to carry out, to adopt, to take
官	guān	Noun: officer, government official
交换	jiāo huàn	Noun: exchange Verb: to exchange, to swap, to switch
临时	lín shí	Adjective: temporary
资源	zī yuán	Noun: resources
顶	dǐng	Noun: top, roof Verb: to carry on the head Adverb: most, extremely, highly Measure Word: for caps, hats, tents, etc.
关闭	guān bì	Verb: to close, to shut
交际	jiāo jì	Noun: communication, social intercourse Verb: socialize
数码	shù mǎ	Noun: number, figure Adjective: digital
总裁	zǒng cái	Noun: general director
观察	guān chá	Noun: observation Verb: to observe, to watch, to survey
教练	jiào liàn	Noun: sports coach, instructor
铃	líng	Noun: bell
墙	qiáng	Noun: wall
输入	shū rù	Verb: to import, to input
总共	zǒng gòng	Adverb: altogether, in total
尽快	jǐn kuài	Adverb: as soon as possible
观点	guān diǎn	Noun: point of view, viewpoint, standpoint
领导	lǐng dǎo	Noun: leader, leadership Verb: to lead
抢	qiǎng	Verb: to grab, to rob
舒适	shū shì	Adjective: comfortable, cosy
综合	zōng hé	Noun: composite Verb: to integrate, to sum up Adjective: synthesized, integrated

尽量	jǐn liàng	Adverb: to the best of one's ability
参考	cān kǎo	Noun: consultation, reference Verb: to consult, to refer to
冻	dòng	Noun: jelly Verb: to freeze, to feel very cold
灵活	líng huó	Adjective: flexible, agile, nimble
枪	qiāng	Noun: gun, spear
媒体	méi tǐ	Noun: media
哎	āi	Expression: to express surprise
惭愧	cán kuì	Adjective: ashamed
洞	dòng	Noun: cave, hole
零件	líng jiàn	Noun: part, component
强调	qiáng diào	Verb: to emphasize, to stress, to underline
吓	xià	Verb: to frighten, to scare
成人	chéng rén	Noun: adult
冠军	guàn jūn	Noun: champion
强烈	qiáng liè	Adjective: intense, strong, violent
瞎	xiā	Adjective: blind Adverb: groundlessly, foolishly, aimlessly
幼儿园	yòu ér yuán	Noun: kindergarten, nursery school
总理	zǒng lǐ	Noun: premier, prime minister
参与	cān yù	Verb: to participate in, to attach oneself to
胶水	jiāo shuǐ	Noun: glue
零食	líng shí	Noun: snack
属于	shǔ yú	Verb: to belong to, to be part of
差距	chā jù	Noun: disparity, gap, difference
观念	guān niàn	Noun: concept, idea, thought
瞧	qiáo	Verb: to look at, to see
优惠	yōu huì	Adjective: preferential, favourable
总算	zǒng suàn	Adverb: finally, in the end, at long last
归纳	guī nà	Verb: to conclude, to sum up, to summarize

操场	cāo chǎng	Noun: playground, sports field
动画片	dòng huà piàn	Noun: cartoon, animation
教训	jiào xùn	Noun: lesson Verb: to teach sbd. a lesson
领域	lǐng yù	Noun: field, domain, area, territory
梳子	shū zi	Noun: comb
下载	xià zài	Verb: to download
悠久	yōu jiǔ	Adjective: long, longstanding
总统	zǒng tǒng	Noun: president (of a country)
淘气	táo qì	Noun: naughty
操心	cāo xīn	Verb: to worry about, to take pains
总之	zǒng zhī	Conjunction: in short, in a word
册	cè	Noun: book, booklet Measure Word: for books
巧妙	qiǎo miào	Adjective: ingenious, clever
县	xiàn	Noun: county
游览	yóu lǎn	Verb: to visit, to go sightseeing
讨价还价	tǎo jià huán jià	Verb: to bargain
流传	liú chuán	Verb: to spread, to circulate, to hand down
悄悄	qiāo qiāo	Adverb: quietly, secretly
甩	shuǎi	Verb: to throw, to swing, to move back and forth
有利	yǒu lì	Adjective: advantageous, beneficial
测验	cè yàn	Noun: test, examination Verb: to test
逗	dòu	Verb: to stay, to pause, to tease
浏览	liú lǎn	Verb: to skim over, to browse, to surf (IT)
切	qiē	Verb: to cut, to chop
现代	xiàn dài	Noun: modern times, the contemporary age
优美	yōu měi	Adjective: fine, graceful
组成	zǔ chéng	Noun: composition Verb: to form, to compose, to constitute

梦想	mèng xiǎng	Noun: dream, wishful thinking Verb: to dream of
管子	guǎn zi	Noun: tube, pipe
届	jiè	Verb: to become due Measure Word: for events, meetings, etc.
流泪	liú lèi	Verb: to shed tears
亲爱	qīn ài	Adjective: dear, beloved
显得	xiǎn de	Verb: to seem, to look, to appear
特色	tè sè	Noun: distinguishing feature Adjective: characteristic
曾经	céng jīng	Adverb: once, former, previously
豆腐	dòu fu	Noun: tofu
勤奋	qín fèn	Adjective: hardworking, diligent
双方	shuāng fāng	Noun: both sides Adjective: bilateral
组合	zǔ hé	Noun: association, combination Verb: to make up, to compose, to constitute
接触	jiē chù	Verb: to touch, to contact, to get in touch with
税	shuì	Noun: tax, duty
接待	jiē dài	Verb: to receive (visitor)
显然	xiǎn rán	Adjective: clear, evident
阻止	zǔ zhǐ	Verb: to prevent, to stop
兑换	duì huàn	Verb: to convert, to exchange
插	chā	Verb: to insert, to stick in
度过	dù guò	Verb: to spend, to pass
广场	guǎng chǎng	Noun: public square
龙	lóng	Noun: dragon
优势	yōu shì	Noun: superiority, dominance, advantage
组织	zǔ zhī	Noun: organisation Verb: to organize
独立	dú lì	Noun: independence Verb: to stand alone Adjective: independent
广大	guǎng dà	Adjective: vast, extensive, widespread

阶段	jiē duàn	Noun: stage, section, phase
亲切	qīn qiè	Noun: friendliness, hospitality Adjective: kind, cordial, amiable
现实	xiàn shí	Noun: reality, actuality Adjective: real, actual
独特	dú tè	Adjective: unique, distinct
广泛	guǎng fàn	Adjective: extensive, wide ranging
漏	lòu	Verb: to leak
亲自	qīn zì	Adverb: personally
显示	xiǎn shì	Noun: display Verb: to show, to display, to demonstrate
醉	zuì	Adjective: intoxicated, drunk
叉子	chā zi	Noun: fork
结构	jié gòu	Noun: structure, makeup, composition
现象	xiàn xiàng	Noun: appearance, phenomenon
拆	chāi	Verb: open, tear down
光滑	guāng huá	Adjective: smooth, sleek, glossy
鲜艳	xiān yàn	Adjective: bright-coloured, colourful
最初	zuì chū	Time: first, initial
产品	chǎn pǐn	Noun: product, goods
断	duàn	Verb: to cut off, to break, to judge, to decide Adverb: absolutely, definitely
光临	guāng lín	Verb: to visit as honourable guest
结合	jié hé	Noun: binding Verb: to combine, to link, to integrate
产生	chǎn shēng	Verb: to produce, to come about
光明	guāng míng	Noun: light, radiance Adjective: light, bright
陆地	lù dì	Noun: land, dry land
青	qīng	Adjective: blue/green
说不定	shuō bu dìng	Adverb: maybe, cannot say for sure
限制	xiàn zhì	Noun: restriction, limit Verb: to restrict, to limit

犹豫	yóu yù	Verb: to hesitate
光盘	guāng pán	Noun: CD, DVD
录取	lù qǔ	Verb: to enrol, being admitted (e.g. university)
说服	shuō fú	Verb: to persuade, to convince
油炸	yóu zhá	Verb: to deep fry
接近	jiē jìn	Verb: to near, to approach, to be close to
青春	qīng chūn	Time: youth, youthfulness
经商	jīng shāng	Verb: to trade, to be in business
陆续	lù xù	Adverb: one after another, bit by bit
清淡	qīng dàn	Adjective: light (food)
尊敬	zūn jìng	Noun: respect, esteem Verb: to respect, to revere
借口	jiè kǒu	Noun: excuse, pretext
录音	lù yīn	Noun: sound recording Verb: to record
预报	yù bào	Noun: forecast
遵守	zūn shǒu	Verb: to abide by, to comply with
长辈	zhǎng bèi	Noun: elder generation
牙齿	yá chǐ	Noun: tooth
堆	duī	Noun: pile, stack, heap Measure Word: for piles of things
规矩	guī ju	Noun: rule, custom, manner, practices
结论	jié lùn	Noun: conclusion
情景	qíng jǐng	Noun: scene, sight, condition, circumstances
对比	duì bǐ	Noun: contrast, comparison Verb: to contrast, to compare
规律	guī lǜ	Noun: law, regular pattern
相处	xiāng chǔ	Verb: to get along with each other
预订	yù dìng	Noun: booking Verb: to book, to subscribe for
常识	cháng shí	Noun: common sense, general knowledge
规模	guī mó	Noun: scale, scope, size, extent

轮流	lún liú	Verb: to alternate, to take turns
撕	sī	Verb: to tear up
相当	xiāng dāng	Verb: be equivalent to Adjective: appropriate Adverb: quite, rather, fairly
长途	cháng tú	Noun: long distance
对待	duì dài	Noun: treatment Verb: to treat, to approach
柜台	guì tái	Noun: (sales) counter, bar
论文	lùn wén	Noun: paper, thesis
请求	qǐng qiú	Noun: request Verb: to request, to ask
丝绸	sī chóu	Noun: silk, silk cloth
相对	xiāng duì	Verb: to face each other Adverb: relatively, comparatively
预防	yù fáng	Noun: prevention, prophylaxis Verb: to prevent
朝	cháo	Noun: dynasty, imperial or royal court Relative Clause: towards, facing
对方	duì fāng	Noun: counterpart, the other side
规则	guī zé	Noun: rule, regulation
节省	jié shěng	Verb: to save, to economize, to use sparingly
落后	luò hòu	Verb: to fall behind, to lag
青少年	qīng shào nián	Noun: young person, teenager
丝毫	sī háo	Adjective: the slightest amount or degree, very little
超级	chāo jí	Relative Clause: super-
吵	chǎo	Verb: to quarrel Adjective: noisy
滚	gǔn	Verb: to boil, to roll
逻辑	luó ji	Noun: logic
轻视	qīng shì	Verb: to look down upon, to contempt
似乎	sì hū	Adverb: apparently, it seems as if, seemingly
相关	xiāng guān	Noun: correlation, dependence Verb: to be interrelated

娱乐	yú lè	Noun: amusement, entertainment Verb: to amuse, to entertain
作品	zuò pǐn	Noun: works (literature, art)
炒	chǎo	Verb: to fry
结实	jiē shi	Adjective: solid, durable, sturdy
耳环	ěr huán	Noun: earring
敏感	mǐn gǎn	Adjective: sensitive, susceptible
抄	chāo	Verb: to copy, to plagiarize
对手	duì shǒu	Noun: opponent, rival
骂	mà	Noun: abuse Verb: to abuse, to curse
情绪	qíng xù	Noun: feeling, mood, sentiment
思考	sī kǎo	Verb: to ponder over, to think over, to reflect upon
项链	xiàng liàn	Noun: necklace
玉米	yù mǐ	Noun: corn, maize
对象	duì xiàng	Noun: lover, partner, target, object
锅	guō	Noun: pot, pan
庆祝	qìng zhù	Verb: to celebrate
与其	yǔ qí	Conjunction: rather than
作为	zuò wéi	Noun: conduct, accomplishment Verb: to accomplish, to act as, to take for Conjunction: as
潮湿	cháo shī	Adjective: wet, damp, moist
私人	sī rén	Noun: private (person) Adjective: private
项目	xiàng mù	Noun: item, project, sports event
语气	yǔ qì	Noun: tone, manner of speaking
吵架	chǎo jià	Noun: quarrel Verb: to quarrel
顿	dùn	Noun: pause Verb: to stop, to pause, to arrange Measure Word: for meals, beatings, etc.
过分	guò fèn	Adjective: excessive, undue

思想	sī xiǎng	Noun: idea, thought, thinking
想念	xiǎng niàn	Verb: to miss, to remember with longing
作文	zuò wén	Noun: composition Verb: to write an essay
吨	dūn	Measure Word: for a ton
球迷	qiú mí	Noun: football fan
彻底	chè dǐ	Adjective: thorough
蹲	dūn	Verb: to squat
结账	jié zhàng	Verb: to pay the bill
象棋	xiàng qí	Noun: Chinese chess
好客	hào kè	Noun: hospitality Verb: to be hospitable Adjective: hospitable, friendly
车库	chē kù	Noun: garage
朵	duǒ	Measure Word: for flowers, clouds, etc.
享受	xiǎng shòu	Noun: enjoyment, pleasure Verb: to enjoy
车厢	chē xiāng	Noun: carriage
过敏	guò mǐn	Noun: allergy Verb: to be allergic
戒指	jiè zhi	Noun: ring (for finger)
娶	qǔ	Verb: to marry (men -> woman)
宿舍	sù shè	Noun: dormitory
相似	xiāng sì	Verb: to resemble, to be similar to
圆	yuán	Noun: circle Adjective: circular, round
趁	chèn	Verb: to take advantage of
躲藏	duǒ cáng	Verb: to hide oneself
过期	guò qī	Verb: to expire, to exceed the time limit
麦克风	mài kè fēng	Noun: microphone
沉默	chén mò	Noun: silence, hush Verb: to keep silent Adjective: silent, uncommunicative

多亏	duō kuī	Adverb: luckily, thanks to
国庆节	Guó qìng jié	Noun: National Day (October 1st)
去世	qù shì	Verb: to pass away, to die
想象	xiǎng xiàng	Noun: imagination Verb: to imagine, to visualize
元旦	Yuán dàn	Noun: New Year's Day
果然	guǒ rán	Adverb: as expected
进步	jìn bù	Noun: progress, improvement Verb: to improve, make progress
馒头	mán tou	Noun: steamed bun
趋势	qū shì	Noun: trend, tendency
碎	suì	Verb: to break into pieces Adjective: broken (into pieces)
称	chēng	Verb: to weigh, to name, to state
多余	duō yú	Adjective: unnecessary, surplus, needless
果实	guǒ shí	Noun: fruits, gains
近代	jìn dài	Time: modern times
取消	qǔ xiāo	Noun: cancellation Verb: to cancel
象征	xiàng zhēng	Noun: symbol Verb: to symbolize, to stand for
承担	chéng dān	Verb: to undertake, to shoulder, to take (responsibility, etc.)
满足	mǎn zú	Verb: to satisfy
劝	quàn	Verb: to advise, to persuade, to encourage
程度	chéng dù	Noun: degree, extent, level
恶劣	è liè	Adjective: very bad, vile, disgusting
哈	hā	Expression: haha, laughter
紧急	jǐn jí	Adjective: urgent, pressing
圈	quān	Noun: circle, ring, loop Measure Word: for loops, laps, etc.
随时	suí shí	Adverb: at all time, at any time
原料	yuán liào	Noun: raw material

成分	chéng fèn	Noun: ingredient, component
进口	jìn kǒu	Noun: import Verb: to import
愿望	yuàn wàng	Noun: desire, wish
海关	hǎi guān	Noun: customs
尽力	jìn lì	Verb: to do all one can
权利	quán lì	Noun: right, privilege
损失	sǔn shī	Noun: loss, damage Verb: to lose, to damage
消费	xiāo fèi	Noun: consumption Verb: to consume
成果	chéng guǒ	Noun: result, achievement, gain
毛病	máo bìng	Noun: defect, fault, trouble
权力	quán lì	Noun: power, authority
学历	xué lì	Noun: educational background
称呼	chēng hu	Noun: name, term of address Verb: to address sbd., to call sbd. (a name)
谨慎	jǐn shèn	Adjective: cautious, prudent
矛盾	máo dùn	Noun: contradiction Adjective: contradictory
全面	quán miàn	Adjective: all-around, overall, comprehensive
所	suǒ	Adverb: actually Measure Word: for houses, buildings, institutions
原则	yuán zé	Noun: principle
海鲜	hǎi xiān	Noun: seafood
金属	jīn shǔ	Noun: metal
锁	suǒ	Noun: lock Verb: to lock up
消化	xiāo huà	Noun: digestion Verb: to digest
成就	chéng jiù	Noun: accomplishment, achievement
冒险	mào xiǎn	Verb: to take a risk
缩短	suō duǎn	Verb: to curtail, to cut down

诚恳	chéng kěn	Adjective: sincere, honest
贸易	mào yì	Noun: trade
确定	què dìng	Verb: to make sure, to define, to determine
成立	chéng lì	Verb: to establish, to set up, to found
发表	fā biǎo	Verb: to issue, to publish
缺乏	quē fá	Noun: shortage Verb: to be short of, to lack
效率	xiào lǜ	Noun: efficiency
划	huá, huà	Noun: Chinese character stroke Verb: to row, to paddle, to cut, to scratch Adjective: being worth it
承认	chéng rèn	Noun: recognition Verb: to admit, to recognize, to acknowledge
发愁	fā chóu	Verb: to worry, to be anxious
确认	què rèn	Noun: confirmation Verb: to confirm, to verify
小麦	xiǎo mài	Noun: wheat
发达	fā dá	Verb: to develop Adjective: developed (country, etc.)
喊	hǎn	Verb: to shout, to yell
发抖	fā dǒu	Verb: to shiver, to shudder, to tremble
小气	xiǎo qi	Adjective: stingy, petty, miserly
晕	yūn	Verb: to pass out, to faint Adjective: dizzy, faint, confused
承受	chéng shòu	Verb: to bear, to endure, to receive
发挥	fā huī	Verb: to develop (skill, ability, idea, etc.), to give play to
魅力	mèi lì	Noun: charm, fascination
群	qún	Measure Word: for group, crowd, etc.
成熟	chéng shú	Adjective: mature
罚款	fá kuǎn	Noun: fine, penalty Verb: to fine
消失	xiāo shī	Verb: to disappear, to fade away
运气	yùn qi	Noun: luck, fate

押金	yā jīn	Noun: deposit, down payment
行业	háng yè	Noun: business, industry, profession
经典	jīng diǎn	Noun: classics, scriptures Adjective: classical
眉毛	méi mao	Noun: eyebrow
销售	xiāo shòu	Noun: sales Verb: to sell
运输	yùn shū	Noun: transport Verb: to transport
程序	chéng xù	Noun: procedure, process, program (IT)
发明	fā míng	Noun: invention Verb: to invent
孝顺	xiào shun	Verb: to be obedient to one's parents
成语	chéng yǔ	Noun: idiom, proverb
发票	fā piào	Noun: invoice, receipt
美术	měi shù	Noun: fine arts, art
燃烧	rán shāo	Verb: to burn, to kindle
运用	yùn yòng	Verb: to use, to utilize
生长	shēng zhǎng	Verb: to grow
称赞	chēng zàn	Verb: to praise, to acclaim, to commend
煤炭	méi tàn	Noun: coal
成长	chéng zhǎng	Verb: to grow up, to mature
难免	nán miǎn	Adjective: hard to avoid, unavoidable
豪华	háo huá	Adjective: luxurious
精力	jīng lì	Noun: energy
绕	rào	Verb: to wind, to coil (around), to go around
太极拳	tài jí quán	Noun: shadowboxing, Taiji
色彩	sè cǎi	Noun: colour, colouring, tint
发言	fā yán	Noun: statement Verb: to speak, to make a speech
台阶	tái jiē	Noun: stairs, step
灾害	zāi hài	Noun: calamity, disaster

翅膀	chì bǎng	Noun: wing
法院	fǎ yuàn	Noun: court of law, court
好奇	hào qí	Adjective: curious, inquisitive
热爱	rè ài	Verb: to love ardently, to adore
太太	tài tai	Noun: wife, Madame, Mrs.
蜜蜂	mì fēng	Noun: honeybee
热烈	rè liè	Adjective: warm (welcome, etc.), enthusiastic
斜	xié	Adjective: inclined, slanting, oblique
再三	zài sān	Adverb: again and again
首	shǒu	Number: first Measure Word: for poems or songs
翻	fān	Verb: to turn over, to flip over
精神	jīng shén	Noun: spirit, mind
赞成	zàn chéng	Verb: to approve of, to agree with
池塘	chí táng	Noun: pool, pond
吃亏	chī kuī	Verb: to suffer losses, to lose out
赞美	zàn měi	Noun: applause, praise Verb: to praise, to admire
持续	chí xù	Verb: to continue, to persist
反而	fǎn ér	Adverb: instead, on the contrary
经营	jīng yíng	Verb: to run, to operate, to engage in (business, etc.)
秘密	mì mì	Noun: secret Adjective: secret, confidential
热心	rè xīn	Noun: enthusiasm Adjective: enthusiastic, ardent, warm-hearted
谈判	tán pàn	Noun: negotiation, talks Verb: to negotiate
歇	xiē	Verb: to rest
嗯	ēn, èn, en	Expression: nonverbal expression of astonishment or approval (depending on tone)
反复	fǎn fù	Adverb: repeatedly
何必	hé bì	Adverb: there is no need to

密切	mì qiè	Adjective: close, intimate
坦率	tǎn shuài	Adjective: frank, open, candid
尺子	chǐ zi	Noun: ruler
合法	hé fǎ	Adjective: legal, legitimate
秘书	mì shū	Noun: secretary
忍不住	rěn bu zhù	Verb: cannot help, unable to bear
冲	chōng	Verb: to flush, to head for
人才	rén cái	Noun: talent, talented person
造成	zào chéng	Verb: to bring about, to create, to cause
充电器	chōng diàn qì	Noun: battery charger
繁荣	fán róng	Adjective: flourishing, prosperous, booming
何况	hé kuàng	Relative Clause: let alone
烫	tàng	Verb: to burn, to iron Adjective: hot (food, etc.)
糟糕	zāo gāo	Adjective: terrible, bad
开水	kāi shuǐ	Noun: boiled water
充分	chōng fèn	Adjective: ample, full, abundant
合理	hé lǐ	Adjective: reasonable, rational
救	jiù	Verb: to relieve, to rescue
面对	miàn duì	Verb: to face, to confront
人口	rén kǒu	Noun: population
重复	chóng fù	Verb: to repeat, to duplicate
范围	fàn wéi	Noun: scope, limit, range
和平	hé píng	Noun: peace
人类	rén lèi	Noun: humanity, mankind
信号	xìn hào	Noun: signal
则	zé	Noun: norm, standard Verb: to follow (rule, etc.) Conjunction: then Measure Word: for written items
充满	chōng mǎn	Verb: brimming with, full of

人民币	rén mín bì	Noun: RMB, Chinese Yuan
桃	táo	Noun: peach
责备	zé bèi	Verb: to blame, to criticize
宠物	chǒng wù	Noun: pet
反映	fǎn yìng	Noun: reflection Verb: to reflect, to mirror
合同	hé tong	Noun: contract
酒吧	jiǔ bā	Noun: bar, pub
面积	miàn jī	Noun: area
人生	rén shēng	Noun: life, human life
逃	táo	Verb: to escape, to run away, to flee
心理	xīn lǐ	Noun: psychology, mentality Adjective: psychological, mental
反应	fǎn yìng	Noun: reaction, response Verb: to react, to respond
核心	hé xīn	Noun: core
救护车	jiù hù chē	Noun: ambulance
面临	miàn lín	Verb: to face sth., to be confronted with
人事	rén shì	Noun: human affairs, personnel
套	tào	Noun: cover Verb: to cover with Measure Word: for sets of things
臭	chòu	Adjective: smelly
反正	fǎn zhèng	Adverb: anyway, whatever happens
合影	hé yǐng	Noun: group photo
逃避	táo bì	Verb: to escape, to avoid, to shirk
信任	xìn rèn	Noun: trust Verb: to trust
丑	chǒu	Noun: clown Adjective: ugly, bad-looking
舅舅	jiù jiu	Noun: uncle (maternal)
欣赏	xīn shǎng	Verb: to enjoy, to appreciate
抽屉	chōu ti	Noun: drawer

方	fāng	Noun: square, direction, side Measure Word: for square things
合作	hé zuò	Noun: cooperation Verb: to cooperate, to work together
苗条	miáo tiao	Adjective: slim, slender, graceful
人物	rén wù	Noun: character, protagonist
看望	kàn wàng	Verb: to visit
抽象	chōu xiàng	Adjective: abstract
妨碍	fáng ài	Verb: to hinder, to obstruct
描写	miáo xiě	Noun: description Verb: to describe, to depict, to portray
窄	zhǎi	Adjective: narrow
方案	fāng àn	Noun: plan, program, scheme
具备	jù bèi	Verb: to possess, to have
人员	rén yuán	Noun: staff, personnel
摘	zhāi	Verb: to pick, to pluck, to take off (glasses, etc.)
怀孕	huái yùn	Noun: pregnancy Verb: to be pregnant
演讲	yǎn jiǎng	Verb: to lecture, to make a speech
恨	hèn	Noun: hate Verb: to hate
巨大	jù dà	Adjective: huge enormous
特殊	tè shū	Adjective: special, unusual
偷	tōu	Verb: to steal
展开	zhǎn kāi	Verb: to unfold, to carry out, to spread out
出版	chū bǎn	Verb: to publish
命令	mìng lìng	Noun: order, command Verb: to order, to command
特征	tè zhēng	Noun: distinctive feature, characteristic
心脏	xīn zàng	Noun: heart
展览	zhǎn lǎn	Noun: exhibition Verb: to exhibit
投入	tóu rù	Verb: to invest, to throw into

仿佛	fǎng fú	Adverb: to seem as if
俱乐部	jù lè bù	Noun: club
名牌	míng pái	Noun: famous brand
粘贴	zhān tiē	Verb: to stick, to affix, to paste
名片	míng piàn	Noun: (business) card
日常	rì cháng	Adjective: daily
疼爱	téng ài	Verb: to love dearly
欧洲	Ōu zhōu	Noun: Europe
主任	zhǔ rèn	Noun: head, director
后果	hòu guǒ	Noun: consequence, aftermath
居然	jū rán	Adverb: unexpectedly
明确	míng què	Adjective: clear, definite, explicit
日程	rì chéng	Noun: schedule
战争	zhàn zhēng	Noun: war
除非	chú fēi	Conjunction: only if, unless
据说	jù shuō	Adverb: it is said, reportedly
名胜古迹	míng shèng gǔ jì	Noun: historical sites and scenic spots
初级	chū jí	Adjective: primary, elementary
方式	fāng shì	Noun: way, pattern, manner
具体	jù tǐ	Adjective: concrete, specific
日历	rì lì	Noun: calendar
提倡	tí chàng	Verb: to promote, to advocate
形成	xíng chéng	Verb: to form, to take shape
涨	zhǎng	Verb: to rise, to go up
抓	zhuā	Verb: to catch, to grab
出口	chū kǒu	Noun: exit, export
明显	míng xiǎn	Adjective: clear, obvious
日期	rì qī	Noun: date
提纲	tí gāng	Noun: key points, outline

行动	xíng dòng	Noun: action, operation Verb: to move, to act
猴子	hóu zi	Noun: monkey
桔子	jú zi	Noun: tangerine
日用品	rì yòng pǐn	Noun: articles for daily use
追	zhuī	Verb: to chase, to pursue
处理	chǔ lǐ	Verb: to deal with, to handle, to cope with
壶	hú	Noun: pot, kettle Measure Word: for bottled liquid
明星	míng xīng	Noun: star, celebrity
账户	zhàng hù	Noun: bank account
重大	zhòng dà	Adjective: significant, great, important
出色	chū sè	Adjective: outstanding, remarkable
蝴蝶	hú dié	Noun: butterfly
命运	mìng yùn	Noun: fate, destiny
体会	tǐ huì	Verb: to know (through experience), to experience
掌握	zhǎng wò	Verb: to grasp, to master, to control

HSK 6

体积	tǐ jī	Noun: volume
保重	bǎo zhòng	Verb: to take care of oneself
储存	chǔ cún	Noun: storage, deposition Verb: to store up, to stockpile
挥霍	huī huò	Verb: to squander (e.g. money) Adjective: agile
可行	kě xíng	Adjective: feasible, practicable
派遣	pài qiǎn	Verb: to send, to dispatch
神气	shén qì	Noun: (facial) expression Adjective: spirited, cocky
挽回	wǎn huí	Verb: to retrieve, to redeem, to save (face)
摇摆	yáo bǎi	Verb: to sway, to swing
指示	zhǐ shì	Noun: instruction Verb: to instruct, to point out
肺	fèi	Noun: lung
荣誉	róng yù	Noun: honour, glory
报仇	bào chóu	Noun: revenge Verb: to revenge, to avenge
处分	chǔ fèn	Noun: punishment Verb: to punish, to discipline
坟墓	fén mù	Noun: tomb
回报	huí bào	Noun: payback Verb: to pay back, to requite
刻不容缓	kè bù róng huǎn	Verb: to demand immediate action
攀登	pān dēng	Verb: to climb, to clamber, to pull oneself up
挽救	wǎn jiù	Verb: to save, to rescue
摇滚	yáo gǔn	Noun: Rock 'n' Roll
指望	zhǐ wàng	Noun: hope Verb: to hope for, to expect, to count on
报酬	bào chou	Noun: reward, pay, remuneration
处境	chǔ jìng	Noun: plight, (unfavourable) situation
粉末	fěn mò	Noun: powder, dust

回避	huí bì	Verb: to avoid, to obviate
客户	kè hù	Noun: client, customer
盘旋	pán xuán	Verb: to spiral, to circle, to hover
惋惜	wǎn xī	Verb: to feel sorry for sbd., to sympathize with
指责	zhǐ zé	Verb: to criticize, to denounce, to accuse
报答	bào dá	Verb: to pay back, to repay
储蓄	chǔ xù	Noun: savings Verb: to deposit money, to save
粉色	fěn sè	Adjective: light pink
回顾	huí gù	Noun: retrospection Verb: to review, to look back
课题	kè tí	Noun: task, topic for study/discussion
畔	pàn	Noun: bank, side, field-path
神圣	shén shèng	Adjective: holy, sacred
万分	wàn fēn	Adverb: very much, extremely
遥控	yáo kòng	Noun: remote control
治安	zhì ān	Noun: public security, law and order
处置	chǔ zhì	Verb: to handle, to deal with, to punish
粉碎	fěn suì	Verb: to break, to smash, to shatter
回收	huí shōu	Verb: to reclaim, to retrieve, to recover
啃	kěn	Verb: to gnaw, to nibble, to bite
判决	pàn jué	Noun: judgment, adjudication Verb: to judge, to sentence
神态	shén tài	Noun: expression, manner
往常	wǎng cháng	Adverb: as one used to do
谣言	yáo yán	Noun: rumour
制裁	zhì cái	Noun: sanctions, punishment Verb: to impose sanction against, to punish
爆发	bào fā	Verb: to erupt, to break out, to explode
触犯	chù fàn	Verb: to offend, to violate
分量	fèn liàng	Noun: weight, quantity

悔恨	huǐ hèn	Noun: remorse, regret Verb: to regret, to be seized with remorse
恳切	kěn qiè	Adjective: earnest, sincere
庞大	páng dà	Adjective: huge, enormous
神仙	shén xiān	Noun: supernatural being, fairy, elf Adjective: immortal
遥远	yáo yuǎn	Adjective: far away, remote, distant
致辞	zhì cí	Verb: to make a speech, to address
报复	bào fù	Noun: revenge, retaliation Verb: to revenge, to retaliate
川流不息	chuān liú bù xī	Verb: to flow in an endless stream
风暴	fēng bào	Noun: storm
毁灭	huǐ miè	Noun: destruction, devastation Verb: to destroy, to ruin
坑	kēng	Noun: pit, hole, tunnel Verb: to cheat, to entrap
抛弃	pāo qì	Verb: to discard, to abandon
审查	shěn chá	Noun: censorship, investigation Verb: to censor, to inspect, to examine
往事	wǎng shì	Noun: past events Time: the past
抱负	bào fù	Noun: ambition, aspiration
穿越	chuān yuè	Verb: to pass though, to cross
封闭	fēng bì	Noun: to seal, to close, to confine
汇报	huì bào	Noun: to report, to give an account of
空洞	kōng dòng	Noun: cavity Adjective: empty, hollow
泡沫	pào mò	Noun: foam, bubble
审理	shěn lǐ	Verb: to try (law), to hear (a case)
妄想	wàng xiǎng	Noun: wishful thinking, a vain hope, delusion Verb: to vainly hope to do sth.
制服	zhì fú	Noun: uniform Verb: to subdue, to bring under control
胡须	hú xū	Noun: beard
曝光	bào guāng	Noun: exposure (photo) Verb: to expose (photo, scandal, etc.)

船舶	chuán bó	Noun: ships, boats
风度	fēng dù	Noun: poise, grace, style
贿赂	huì lù	Noun: bribe Verb: to bribe
空前绝后	kōng qián jué hòu	Adjective: unmatched, unique
审美	shěn měi	Noun: taste, appreciation of the beauty Adjective: aesthetic
微不足道	wēi bù zú dào	Adjective: insignificant, negligible
要点	yào diǎn	Noun: main point, essential
治理	zhì lǐ	Verb: to govern, to administer
暴力	bào lì	Noun: violence
传达	chuán dá	Verb: to pass on, to transmit
风光	fēng guāng	Noun: scene, sight, landscape, good reputation
会晤	huì wù	Noun: meeting, contact Verb: to meet
空想	kōng xiǎng	Noun: daydream, fantasy, phantasm Verb: to daydream, to build castles in the air
培育	péi yù	Noun: culture Verb: to cultivate, to breed, to foster
审判	shěn pàn	Noun: trial Verb: put (sbd.) on trial
威风	wēi fēng	Noun: power and prestige Adjective: majestic, awe-inspiring
要命	yào mìng	Adjective: extremely, serious
智力	zhì lì	Noun: intelligence
暴露	bào lù	Verb: to expose, to reveal
传单	chuán dān	Noun: leaflet, flyer
封建	fēng jiàn	Noun: feudalism Adjective: feudal
昏迷	hūn mí	Noun: coma, stupor Adjective: unconscious
空虚	kōng xū	Noun: emptiness Adjective: empty, hollow
配备	pèi bèi	Noun: equipment Verb: to equip, to allocate

渗透	shèn tòu	Noun: osmosis, infiltration Verb: to permeate, to infiltrate
微观	wēi guān	Adjective: microscopic
要素	yào sù	Noun: essential factor, key element
传授	chuán shòu	Verb: to pass on, to teach, to impart
锋利	fēng lì	Adjective: sharp (e.g. knife)
浑身	hún shēn	Adverb: from head to foot, all over
孔	kǒng	Noun: hole, aperture, opening
配偶	pèi ǒu	Noun: spouse, partner
慎重	shèn zhòng	Adjective: cautious, careful, prudent
危机	wēi jī	Noun: crisis
耀眼	yào yǎn	Adjective: dazzling, glaring
滞留	zhì liú	Verb: stand still, to detain
报销	bào xiāo	Verb: write-off, wipe out, apply for reimbursement
喘气	chuǎn qì	Verb: to pant, to gasp, to breathe deeply
丰满	fēng mǎn	Adjective: plump, well-rounded, plentiful
混合	hùn hé	Verb: to mix, to blend
恐吓	kǒng hè	Verb: to threaten, to frighten
配套	pèi tào	Verb: to form a complete set
牲畜	shēng chù	Noun: livestock, domesticated animals
威力	wēi lì	Noun: might, formidable power
野蛮	yě mán	Noun: barbarous, uncivilized, wild
智能	zhì néng	Noun: intelligence, brainpower Adjective: intelligent
蚂蚁	mǎ yǐ	Noun: ant
串	chuàn	Verb: to string together, to connect Measure Word: for rows, strings, skewers etc.
风气	fēng qì	Noun: common practice, atmosphere
混乱	hùn luàn	Noun: chaos, confusion, disorder Adjective: chaotic, disorderly, unorganized
恐惧	kǒng jù	Noun: fear, dread, phobia

盆地	pén dì	Noun: basin (geography), bowl, pan
生存	shēng cún	Noun: existence Verb: to exist, to survive
威望	wēi wàng	Noun: prestige
野心	yě xīn	Noun: ambition
志气	zhì qì	Noun: aspiration, ambition, spirit
愤怒	fèn nù	Adjective: angry
田野	tián yě	Noun: field, open land
爆炸	bào zhà	Noun: explosion Verb: to explode, to blow up
床单	chuáng dān	Noun: bed sheet
风趣	fēng qù	Noun: humour Adjective: humorous, witty
混淆	hùn xiáo	Verb: to confuse, to mix up
空白	kòng bái	Noun: blank space, gap
烹饪	pēng rèn	Noun: cooking, culinary arts Verb: to cook
生机	shēng jī	Noun: chance of survival, vitality
威信	wēi xìn	Noun: prestige and public reliance (government, etc.)
智商	zhì shāng	Noun: IQ
悲哀	bēi āi	Adjective: grieved, sorrowful
创立	chuàng lì	Verb: to found, to establish
丰盛	fēng shèng	Adjective: rich, sumptuous
混浊	hùn zhuó	Adjective: turbid, dirty
空隙	kòng xì	Noun: gap, crack
捧	pěng	Verb: to hold up with both hands, to flatter
生理	shēng lǐ	Noun: physiology
违背	wéi bèi	Noun: to disobey, to violate, to go against
一度	yí dù	Adverb: once, for some time
致使	zhì shǐ	Verb: to cause, to result in
雄伟	xióng wěi	Adjective: grand, magnificent

卑鄙	bēi bǐ	Adjective: mean, despicable
创新	chuàng xīn	Noun: innovation Verb: to bring forth new ideas, to innovate
丰收	fēng shōu	Verb: have a good harvest
活该	huó gāi	Verb: to serve sbd. right Adverb: deservedly
口气	kǒu qì	Noun: tone, manner (of saying something)
劈	pī	Verb: to hack, to chop, to cleave
声明	shēng míng	Noun: statement, declaration Verb: to state, to declare
维持	wéi chí	Verb: to keep, to maintain, to preserve
一帆风顺	yì fān fēng shùn	Adjective: smooth
制约	zhì yuē	Noun: restriction Verb: to restrict, to condition
悲惨	bēi cǎn	Adjective: tragic, miserable
创业	chuàng yè	Verb: to start an enterprise, to do pioneering work
封锁	fēng suǒ	Verb: to blockade, to seal off
活力	huó lì	Noun: energy, vitality, vigour
口腔	kǒu qiāng	Noun: oral cavity
批发	pī fā	Noun: wholesale Verb: to wholesale
声势	shēng shì	Noun: momentum
唯独	wéi dú	Adverb: only, just, alone
一贯	yí guàn	Adjective: consistent, constant, all along
制止	zhì zhǐ	Verb: to curb, to stop, to prevent
真理	zhēn lǐ	Noun: truth
北极	běi jí	Location: North Pole
创作	chuàng zuò	Noun: creation, creative work Verb: to create, to produce, to write
风土人情	fēng tǔ rén qíng	Noun: local conditions and customs
火箭	huǒ jiàn	Noun: rocket
口头	kǒu tóu	Adjective: verbal, spoken, oral

批判	pī pàn	Verb: to criticize
生疏	shēng shū	Adjective: strange, unfamiliar, out of practice
为难	wéi nán	Verb: to feel embarrassed, to feel awkward
依旧	yī jiù	Adverb: as before, still like before
忠诚	zhōng chéng	Noun: loyalty Adjective: loyal, devoted
被动	bèi dòng	Adjective: passive
吹牛	chuī niú	Verb: to brag, to boast
风味	fēng wèi	Noun: flavour or style typical for a region
火焰	huǒ yàn	Noun: flame, blaze
口音	kǒu yīn	Noun: accent
疲惫	pí bèi	Adjective: exhausted, tired
生态	shēng tài	Noun: ecology
为期	wéi qī	Verb: be done by a definite date
一举两得	yì jǔ liǎng dé	Verb: hit two birds with one stone
终点	zhōng diǎn	Noun: destination, end point, terminal
磁带	cí dài	Noun: magnetic tape
枕头	zhěn tou	Noun: pillow
备份	bèi fèn	Adjective: backup
吹捧	chuī pěng	Verb: to flatter, to lavish praise on
逢	féng	Verb: to meet by chance, to come across
火药	huǒ yào	Noun: gunpowder
皮革	pí gé	Noun: leather
生物	shēng wù	Noun: organism, living thing
维生素	wéi shēng sù	Noun: vitamin
依据	yī jù	Noun: basis, grounds Adverb: according to, based on
中断	zhōng duàn	Verb: to break off, to interrupt, to discontinue
被告	bèi gào	Noun: defendant
锤	chuí	Noun: hammer Verb: to hammer

奉献	fèng xiàn	Noun: dedication Verb: to dedicate, to devote
货币	huò bì	Noun: currency, money
枯燥	kū zào	Adjective: boring, dry, dull
疲倦	pí juàn	Noun: fatigue Adjective: tired, sleepy
生效	shēng xiào	Verb: to take effect, to come into effect
依靠	yī kào	Noun: backing, support Verb: to rely on, to depend on
终究	zhōng jiū	Adverb: in the end, after all
贝壳	bèi ké	Noun: shell
垂直	chuí zhí	Adjective: vertical, perpendicular
否决	fǒu jué	Noun: veto Verb: to veto, to reject, to overrule
苦尽甘来	kǔ jìn gān lái	Expression: bitterness finishes, sweetness begins
屁股	pì gu	Noun: buttocks, bottom
生锈	shēng xiù	Noun: corrosion Verb: to rust, to corrode
依赖	yī lài	Verb: to depend on, to be dependent on
中立	zhōng lì	Noun: neutrality Adjective: neutral
背叛	bèi pàn	Verb: to betray
纯粹	chún cuì	Adjective: pure, simple, absolute
夫妇	fū fù	Noun: (married) couple, husband and wife
基地	jī dì	Noun: base, military base
挎	kuà	Verb: to carry (on/over arm)
譬如	pì rú	Adverb: for example, for instance
生育	shēng yù	Verb: to bear, to give birth to, procreate
委员	wěi yuán	Noun: committee member, commissioner
一流	yī liú	Adjective: best, top quality
抗议	kàng yì	Verb: to protest
背诵	bèi sòng	Verb: to recite, to repeat from memory

纯洁	chún jié	Verb: to purify Adjective: pure, chaste, honest
夫人	fū rén	Noun: lady, madam
机动	jī dòng	Adjective: motorized, power-driven, flexible, mobile
跨	kuà	Verb: to step across, to stride over
偏差	piān chā	Noun: deviation, error
声誉	shēng yù	Noun: reputation, fame
伪造	wěi zào	Verb: to forge, to fake
终身	zhōng shēn	Adjective: lifelong Adverb: all one's life
铜	tóng	Noun: copper
政策	zhèng cè	Noun: policy
备忘录	bèi wàng lù	Noun: memo, written reminder
敷衍	fū yǎn	Verb: to do sth. half-heartedly, to elaborate on
饥饿	jī è	Noun: hunger, starvation Adjective: hungry, starving
快活	kuài huo	Adjective: happy, cheerful
偏见	piān jiàn	Noun: prejudice
省会	shěng huì	Noun: provincial capital
畏惧	wèi jù	Verb: to fear, to dread, to be afraid of
一目了然	yí mù liǎo rán	Adjective: obvious
忠实	zhōng shí	Adjective: faithful, trustworthy
奔波	bēn bō	Verb: to rush about
慈祥	cí xiáng	Adjective: kind
幅度	fú dù	Noun: range, extent
激发	jī fā	Verb: to arouse, to excite, to inspire
宽敞	kuān chang	Adjective: spacious
偏僻	piān pì	Adjective: remote, out-of-the-way
盛产	shèng chǎn	Verb: to abound, to teem with
一如既往	yì rú jì wǎng	Adverb: as before, just as in the past

衷心	zhōng xīn	Adjective: wholehearted, heartfelt
选举	xuǎn jǔ	Noun: election Verb: to elect
奔驰	bēn chí	Verb: to run quickly, to move fast
雌雄	cí xióng	Adjective: male and female
符号	fú hào	Noun: symbol, mark, sign
机构	jī gòu	Noun: mechanism, organization, institution
款待	kuǎn dài	Verb: to entertain hospitably, to treat hospitably
偏偏	piān piān	Adverb: contrary to expectations, against one's wish
胜负	shèng fù	Noun: victory or defeat
未免	wèi miǎn	Adverb: rather, a bit too
衣裳	yī shang	Noun: clothes
中央	zhōng yāng	Noun: centre, central authorities Adjective: central
本能	běn néng	Noun: instinct
刺	cì	Noun: thorn, splinter Verb: to stab
福利	fú lì	Noun: well-being, welfare
款式	kuǎn shì	Noun: design, style, pattern
盛开	shèng kāi	Verb: to bloom
慰问	wèi wèn	Noun: consolation, greetings Verb: to express sympathy
一丝不苟	yì sī bù gǒu	Adjective: meticulous, not one hair out of place
终止	zhōng zhǐ	Verb: to stop, to end
皇帝	huáng dì	Noun: emperor
本钱	běn qián	Noun: capital (money)
伺候	cì hòu	Verb: to serve, to wait on
俘虏	fú lǔ	Noun: captive, prisoner Verb: to capture, to arrest
基金	jī jīn	Noun: fund
筐	kuāng	Noun: basket

片刻	piàn kè	Noun: moment, short period of time
盛情	shèng qíng	Noun: magnificent hospitality, great kindness
卫星	wèi xīng	Noun: satellite
依托	yī tuō	Verb: to rely on, to depend on
肿瘤	zhǒng liú	Noun: tumour
本人	běn rén	Pronoun: I, myself Adverb: oneself, personal
次品	cì pǐn	Noun: substandard products, defective goods
服气	fú qì	Verb: to be convinced, to accept
激励	jī lì	Verb: to encourage, to motivate
框架	kuàng jià	Noun: frame, framework
漂浮	piāo fú	Verb: to float, to drift Adjective: superficial, showy
盛行	shèng xíng	Verb: to prevail, to be in vogue
一向	yí xiàng	Adverb: always, all along, constantly
种子	zhǒng zi	Noun: seed
皇后	huáng hòu	Noun: empress
本身	běn shēn	Pronoun: itself, in itself
次序	cì xù	Noun: sequence, order
福气	fú qi	Noun: good fortune, felicity
机灵	jī ling	Adjective: clever, quick-witted
旷课	kuàng kè	Verb: to skip class
飘扬	piāo yáng	Verb: to wave, to flutter, to fly
师范	shī fàn	Noun: teacher training Adjective: pedagogical
温带	wēn dài	Noun: temperate zone
种族	zhǒng zú	Noun: race, ethnicity
服从	fú cóng	Verb: to obey, to submit
本事	běn shi	Noun: ability, skill
丛	cóng	Noun: collection, tussock, thicket Measure Word: for some plants

辐射	fú shè	Noun: radiation Verb: to radiate
机密	jī mì	Noun: secret Adjective: secret, classified
况且	kuàng qiě	Conjunction: moreover, in addition
拼搏	pīn bó	Verb: to work as hard as possible
施加	shī jiā	Verb: to exert (pressure)
温和	wēn hé	Adjective: moderate, mild, temperate
遗产	yí chǎn	Noun: heritage, legacy
众所周知	zhòng suǒ zhōu zhī	Expression: as everyone knows
矿产	kuàng chǎn	Noun: minerals
腐败	fǔ bài	Noun: corruption Adjective: corrupt, rotten
激情	jī qíng	Noun: passion, enthusiasm
亏待	kuī dài	Verb: to treat sbd. unfairly
拼命	pīn mìng	Adjective: with all one has, at all costs
尸体	shī tǐ	Noun: dead body, cadaver
文凭	wén píng	Noun: diploma
遗传	yí chuán	Noun: heredity, inheritance Verb: to inherit, to transmit
重心	zhòng xīn	Noun: centre of gravity, central core
侄子	zhí zi	Noun: nephew
通讯	tōng xùn	Noun: communication, news report
笨拙	bèn zhuō	Adjective: clumsy
凑合	còu he	Verb: to gather together, to improvise Adverb: passable, not too bad
腐烂	fǔ làn	Verb: to rot, to perish
讥笑	jī xiào	Noun: ironical smile Verb: to sneer at, to ridicule
亏损	kuī sǔn	Noun: deficit, loss Verb: to lose, to make a loss
贫乏	pín fá	Adjective: poor, lacking, insufficient
失误	shī wù	Noun: lapse, mistake, fault

文物	wén wù	Noun: cultural relic
疑惑	yí huò	Noun: doubt Verb: to doubt
州	zhōu	Noun: province, state (e.g. of US)
崩溃	bēng kuì	Noun: breakdown Verb: to break down, to collapse
粗鲁	cū lǔ	Adjective: rude, rough, impolite
腐蚀	fǔ shí	Noun: corrosion, corruption Verb: to corrode, to rot, to corrupt
机械	jī xiè	Noun: machine Adjective: mechanical, inflexible
频繁	pín fán	Adverb: frequently, often
施展	shī zhǎn	Verb: to give full play, to put to good use
文献	wén xiàn	Noun: document, literature
遗留	yí liú	Verb: to leave behind, to hand down (to next generation)
舟	zhōu	Noun: boat
甭	béng	Adverb: need not
窜	cuàn	Verb: to flee, to escape
腐朽	fǔ xiǔ	Adjective: rotten, decayed
基因	jī yīn	Noun: gene
捆绑	kǔn bǎng	Verb: to bind, to bind up
贫困	pín kùn	Noun: poverty Adjective: poor
失踪	shī zōng	Verb: to disappear, to be missing
文雅	wén yǎ	Adjective: elegant, refined
仪器	yí qì	Noun: instrument, apparatus
粥	zhōu	Noun: porridge
统治	tǒng zhì	Noun: regime, government Verb: to rule, to govern
蹦	bèng	Verb: to jump
摧残	cuī cán	Verb: to devastate, to ruin
抚养	fǔ yǎng	Verb: to foster, to bring up

机遇	jī yù	Noun: opportunity
扩充	kuò chōng	Verb: to expand, to enlarge
频率	pín lǜ	Noun: frequency
拾	shí	Verb: to pick up Number: 10 (in banks)
文艺	wén yì	Noun: literature and art
遗失	yí shī	Verb: to lose, to miss
周边	zhōu biān	Noun: periphery, rim
迸发	bèng fā	Verb: to burst out, to gush, to spurt
脆弱	cuì ruò	Adjective: flimsy, weak, frail
机智	jī zhì	Noun: tact, alertness Adjective: quick-witted, tactful, resourceful
扩散	kuò sàn	Noun: spread, diffusion Verb: to spread, to diffuse
品尝	pǐn cháng	Noun: sample Verb: to sample, to taste
识别	shí bié	Verb: to identify, to distinguish
问世	wèn shì	Verb: to be published, to come out
仪式	yí shì	Noun: ceremony, ritual
周密	zhōu mì	Adjective: careful, thorough
逼迫	bī pò	Verb: to force, to compel
搓	cuō	Verb: to rub the hands together
辅助	fǔ zhù	Noun: auxiliary Verb: to assist
即便	jí biàn	Conjunction: even if, even though
扩张	kuò zhāng	Noun: expansion Verb: to expand, to broaden
品德	pǐn dé	Noun: moral character
窝	wō	Noun: nest Measure Word: for broods, nests, etc.
以便	yǐ biàn	Conjunction: so that, in order to
周年	zhōu nián	Noun: anniversary
拨	bō	Verb: to push around with hand or foot

鼻涕	bí tì	Noun: nasal mucus, snot
磋商	cuō shāng	Noun: consultation Verb: to consult, to discuss, to negotiate
副	fù	Adjective: deputy, vice- Measure Word: for pairs, sets, etc.
级别	jí bié	Noun: rank, level, grade
啦	la	Particle: to end a sentence
时常	shí cháng	Adverb: often, frequently
乌黑	wū hēi	Adjective: jet-black
以免	yǐ miǎn	Conjunction: in order to avoid, for fear that
周期	zhōu qī	Noun: period, cycle
比方	bǐ fang	Noun: analogy, instance
挫折	cuò zhé	Noun: setback, reverse, defeat
负担	fù dān	Noun: burden Verb: to bear a burden
疾病	jí bìng	Noun: disease, sickness
喇叭	lǎ ba	Noun: horn (car, etc.), loudspeaker, trumpet
品质	pǐn zhì	Noun: quality
时而	shí ér	Adverb: occasionally, from time to time
污蔑	wū miè	Verb: to slander, to defile
以往	yǐ wǎng	Adverb: in the past, formerly
周折	zhōu zhé	Noun: complication, setback
比喻	bǐ yù	Noun: metaphor
搭	dā	Verb: to put up, to build, to take (boat, bus, train, etc.)
覆盖	fù gài	Verb: to cover, to lay over
嫉妒	jí dù	Noun: jealousy Verb: to be jealous, to envy Adjective: jealous
来历	lái lì	Noun: history, origin, source
平凡	píng fán	Adjective: common, ordinary
时光	shí guāng	Time: time, days

诬陷	wū xiàn	Verb: to plant false evidence against sbd.
以至	yǐ zhì	Conjunction: down to, up to, to such an extent as to
周转	zhōu zhuǎn	Noun: turnover Verb: to circulate, to revolve
比重	bǐ zhòng	Noun: proportion, specific weight
搭档	dā dàng	Noun: partner Verb: to cooperate, to work together
附和	fù hè	Verb: to repeat what others say, to echo
极端	jí duān	Adjective: extreme, radical, utmost
来源	lái yuán	Noun: source, origin
评估	píng gū	Noun: evaluation, assessment Verb: to evaluate, to assess
实惠	shí huì	Noun: tangible benefit, material advantage Adjective: advantageous
无比	wú bǐ	Adjective: incomparable, matchless
以致	yǐ zhì	Conjunction: as a result, so that, consequently
皱纹	zhòu wén	Noun: wrinkle
臂	bì	Noun: arm
搭配	dā pèi	Verb: to arrange, to match
复活	fù huó	Noun: resurrection Verb: to bring back to life, to revive
急功近利	jí gōng jìn lì	Verb: looking only for fast success
栏目	lán mù	Noun: column
评论	píng lùn	Noun: commentary, review Verb: to comment on, to discuss
时机	shí jī	Noun: moment of opportunity, fortunate timing
无偿	wú cháng	Adjective: free, free of charge
亦	yì	Adverb: also
昼夜	zhòu yè	Time: day and night, 24 hours
弊病	bì bìng	Noun: disadvantage, malpractice, ulcer
答辩	dá biàn	Noun: plea (law) Verb: to reply to a charge

附件	fù jiàn	Noun: enclosure, attachment, appendix
籍贯	jí guàn	Noun: native place, place of ancestry
懒惰	lǎn duò	Adjective: lazy, idle
平面	píng miàn	Noun: plane, flat surface, plane surface
实力	shí lì	Noun: strength
无耻	wú chǐ	Adjective: shameless, infamous, dishonourable
翼	yì	Noun: wing, flank Verb: to assist; to help (an emperor)
株	zhū	Noun: tree trunk, tree root, plant Measure Word: for trees or plants
舌头	shé tou	Noun: tongue
达成	dá chéng	Verb: to reach (agreement), to accomplish
附属	fù shǔ	Noun: subsidiary Adjective: subordinate, attached
即将	jí jiāng	Verb: to be about to Adverb: soon, right away
狼狈	láng bèi	Verb: to be in a difficult/embarrassing situation
平坦	píng tǎn	Adjective: flat, level, even
实施	shí shī	Verb: to carry out, to enforce, to implement
异常	yì cháng	Adjective: exceptional, unusual, abnormal
诸位	zhū wèi	Pronoun: everyone, Ladies and Gentlemen
弊端	bì duān	Noun: malpractice, abuse
答复	dá fù	Verb: to answer, to reply
腹泻	fù xiè	Noun: diarrhoea Verb: to have the runs
急剧	jí jù	Adjective: rapid, sudden, abrupt
平行	píng xíng	Adjective: parallel, simultaneous, at the same level
时事	shí shì	Noun: current affairs, present situation
无动于衷	wú dòng yú zhōng	Adjective: aloof, indifferent, unconcerned
毅力	yì lì	Noun: perseverance, willpower
逐年	zhú nián	Adverb: year after year

闭塞	bì sè	Verb: to block, to close up, to stop up Adjective: inaccessible, unenlightened
打包	dǎ bāo	Verb: to pack, to wrap
复兴	fù xīng	Noun: rebirth Verb: to revive, to renew
急切	jí qiè	Adjective: eager, impatient
捞	lāo	Verb: to fish up, to dredge up
平原	píng yuán	Noun: plain, field
实事求是	shí shì qiú shì	Verb: to be practical and realistic
无非	wú fēi	Adverb: nothing but, only, simply
意料	yì liào	Noun: anticipation, expectation Verb: to anticipate, to expect
拄	zhǔ	Verb: to lean on (a stick)
打官司	dǎ guān si	Verb: to sue, to go to court
赋予	fù yǔ	Verb: to assign, to give, to endow
集团	jí tuán	Noun: group, bloc, corporation
唠叨	láo dao	Verb: to chatter, to prattle, to nag
屏障	píng zhàng	Noun: protective screen, barrier, shield
石油	shí yóu	Noun: oil, petroleum
无精打采	wú jīng dǎ cǎi	Adjective: dispirited, listless, in low spirits
毅然	yì rán	Adverb: firmly, resolutely
主办	zhǔ bàn	Verb: to organize, to sponsor, to host
鞭策	biān cè	Verb: to urge on
打击	dǎ jī	Noun: blow, hit Verb: to strike, to hit, to attack
富裕	fù yù	Noun: richness, affluence Adjective: prosperous, rich, affluent
极限	jí xiàn	Noun: limit, utmost
牢固	láo gù	Adjective: solid, firm, secure, strong
坡	pō	Noun: slope
实质	shí zhì	Noun: essence, substance
意识	yì shí	Noun: consciousness, awareness Verb: to be aware of

主导	zhǔ dǎo	Verb: to lead, to manage Adjective: leading, predominant
边疆	biān jiāng	Noun: border area
打架	dǎ jià	Noun: fight, fistfight Verb: to fight, to scuffle
吉祥	jí xiáng	Adjective: lucky, auspicious
牢骚	láo sāo	Noun: complaint, grievance
泼	pō	Verb: to splash, to spill
意图	yì tú	Noun: intention, purpose
主管	zhǔ guǎn	Noun: person in charge, boss Verb: to be in charge of
恐怖	kǒng bù	Adjective: terrible, fearful, frightening
边界	biān jiè	Noun: border, boundary
打量	dǎ liang	Verb: to take measure of, to suppose, to reckon
改良	gǎi liáng	Verb: to improve
急于求成	jí yú qiú chéng	Verb: to demand quick results
乐趣	lè qù	Noun: joy, delight, pleasure
颇	pō	Adverb: very, pretty
十足	shí zú	Adjective: complete, hundred percent, full of
无赖	wú lài	Noun: rascal, hoodlum, hooligan
意味着	yì wèi zhe	Verb: to mean, to imply, to signify
主流	zhǔ liú	Noun: main stream (of river), main aspect of a matter
边境	biān jìng	Noun: border, frontier
打猎	dǎ liè	Noun: hunt Verb: to go hunting
盖章	gài zhāng	Verb: to affix a seal, to stamp
及早	jí zǎo	Adverb: as soon as possible
乐意	lè yì	Verb: to be willing to, to be ready to
迫不及待	pò bù jí dài	Verb: to be too impatient to wait, to brook no delay
使命	shǐ mìng	Noun: mission, task

无理取闹	wú lǐ qǔ nào	Verb: to make trouble without reason, to be deliberately awkward
意向	yì xiàng	Noun: intention, purpose, disposition
主权	zhǔ quán	Noun: sovereignty
神经	shén jīng	Noun: nerve
边缘	biān yuán	Noun: edge, fringe, brink
打仗	dǎ zhàng	Verb: to go to war, to fight, to make war
尴尬	gān gà	Adjective: embarrassed, awkward
急躁	jí zào	Adjective: impatient, irritable, impetuous
雷达	léi dá	Noun: radar
迫害	pò hài	Noun: persecution Verb: to persecute
势必	shì bì	Adverb: certainly will, is bound to
无能为力	wú néng wéi lì	Adjective: powerless, helpless
意志	yì zhì	Noun: will, determination
摊	tān	Noun: vendor's stand
大不了	dà bu liǎo	Adverb: at worst, if worst comes to worst
干旱	gān hàn	Noun: drought Adjective: arid, dry
给予	jǐ yǔ	Verb: to give, to render, to present, to accord
类似	lèi sì	Adjective: similar, analogous
破例	pò lì	Verb: to make an exception
世代	shì dài	Noun: generation, era
无穷无尽	wú qióng wú jìn	Adjective: endless, boundless
助理	zhù lǐ	Noun: assistant
扁	biǎn	Adjective: flat
大臣	dà chén	Noun: minister (in monarchy)
干扰	gān rǎo	Noun: obstruction Verb: to interfere, to disturb
继承	jì chéng	Verb: to inherit, to carry on, to succeed
魄力	pò lì	Noun: courage, daring, boldness

示范	shì fàn	Noun: demonstration Verb: to demonstrate, to show how to do sth.
无微不至	wú wēi bú zhì	Adjective: meticulously
阴谋	yīn móu	Noun: plot, conspiracy, machination
注射	zhù shè	Noun: injection Verb: to inject, to shoot
贬低	biǎn dī	Verb: to belittle, to degrade, to depreciate
大伙儿	dà huǒ r	Pronoun: everyone, all of us
干涉	gān shè	Noun: interference Verb: to interfere, to intervene
季度	jì dù	Time: quarter, 3 months
冷酷	lěng kù	Adjective: grim, hard-hearted, callous
扑	pū	Verb: to throw oneself on, to pounce
释放	shì fàng	Verb: to release, to set free
无忧无虑	wú yōu wú lǜ	Adjective: carefree and without worries
音响	yīn xiǎng	Noun: sound, stereo, acoustics
注视	zhù shì	Verb: to watch attentively, to gaze at
扣	kòu	Noun: button Verb: to deduct
贬义	biǎn yì	Noun: derogatory sense
忌讳	jì huì	Noun: taboo Verb: to abstain from
冷却	lěng què	Noun: cooling Verb: to cool
铺	pū	Verb: to spread, to extend, to pave, to lay
是非	shì fēi	Noun: quarrel, dispute Adjective: right or wrong
无知	wú zhī	Noun: ignorance Adjective: ignorant, innocent
隐蔽	yǐn bì	Verb: to conceal, to hide
注释	zhù shì	Noun: annotation, note Verb: to annotate, to comment
遍布	biàn bù	Verb: to be found throughout
大肆	dà sì	Adjective: wantonly, without restraint

干预	gān yù	Noun: intervention Verb: to intervene, to meddle
计较	jì jiào	Verb: to haggle, to bicker
愣	lèng	Verb: to look distracted Adjective: distracted Adverb: rashly
普及	pǔ jí	Verb: to popularize Adjective: popular, universally available
事故	shì gù	Noun: accident
舞蹈	wǔ dǎo	Noun: dance
引导	yǐn dǎo	Noun: introduction Verb: to guide, to lead, to direct
助手	zhù shǒu	Noun: assistant, helper
变故	biàn gù	Noun: accident, unforeseen event
大体	dà tǐ	Adverb: in general, roughly, more or less
感慨	gǎn kǎi	Verb: to sigh with emotion
寂静	jì jìng	Adjective: silent, quiet
黎明	lí míng	Noun: dawn, daybreak
朴实	pǔ shí	Adjective: plain, simple
事迹	shì jì	Noun: deed, achievement
侮辱	wǔ rǔ	Verb: to insult, to humiliate, to dishonour
隐患	yǐn huàn	Noun: hidden danger
铸造	zhù zào	Noun: casting, founding Verb: to cast, to found
辩护	biàn hù	Verb: to speak in defence of, to defend
大意	dà yi	Noun: general idea, main idea
感染	gǎn rǎn	Noun: infection Verb: to infect, to influence
季军	jì jūn	Noun: bronze medallist
理睬	lǐ cǎi	Verb: to pay attention to, to show interest in
瀑布	pù bù	Noun: waterfall
事件	shì jiàn	Noun: event, happening, incident
武侠	wǔ xiá	Noun: martial arts chivalry (Chinese genre)

隐瞒	yǐn mán	Verb: to conceal, to hide, to cover up
驻扎	zhù zhā	Verb: to station (troops)
辩解	biàn jiě	Verb: to provide an explanation, to justify, to defend
大致	dà zhì	Adverb: roughly, more or less
干劲	gàn jìn	Noun: enthusiasm, vigour, drive
里程碑	lǐ chéng bēi	Noun: milestone
欺负	qī fu	Verb: to bully, to intimidate
武装	wǔ zhuāng	Noun: military, arms, equipment Verb: to arm, to equip
引擎	yǐn qíng	Noun: engine
住宅	zhù zhái	Noun: residence, tenement
倘若	tǎng ruò	Conjunction: if, in case
便利	biàn lì	Adjective: convenient, easy
歹徒	dǎi tú	Noun: gangster, evil-doer
扛	káng	Verb: to carry on the shoulder
技巧	jì qiǎo	Noun: skill, technique
礼节	lǐ jié	Noun: etiquette, manners
凄凉	qī liáng	Adjective: desolate, dreary, lonely
视力	shì lì	Noun: eyesight
饮食	yǐn shí	Noun: food and drink
注重	zhù zhòng	Verb: to emphasize, to attach importance to
变迁	biàn qiān	Noun: changes, vicissitudes
逮捕	dài bǔ	Noun: arrest Verb: to arrest, to apprehend
纲领	gāng lǐng	Noun: guiding principle, program
寄托	jì tuō	Verb: to place (hope, etc.) on, consign
理所当然	lǐ suǒ dāng rán	Verb: to go without saying Adjective: inevitable and right
欺骗	qī piàn	Verb: to deceive, to cheat
势力	shì li	Noun: force, power, influence

务必	wù bì	Adverb: to be sure to, must
隐私	yǐn sī	Noun: one's secrets, private matters
著作	zhù zuò	Noun: literary work, book, writings Noun: to write
辨认	biàn rèn	Verb: to recognize, to identify
代价	dài jià	Noun: price, cost
港口	gǎng kǒu	Noun: port, harbour
理直气壮	lǐ zhí qì zhuàng	Verb: to be in the right and self-confident
期望	qī wàng	Noun: hope, expectation Verb: to hope, to expect
逝世	shì shì	Verb: to pass away, to die
误差	wù chā	Noun: difference, error, inaccuracy (in measuring)
引用	yǐn yòng	Verb: to quote, to cite
拽	zhuài	Verb: to drag, to haul
团圆	tuán yuán	Verb: to reunite
便条	biàn tiáo	Noun: (informal) note
代理	dài lǐ	Noun: agency, representation Verb: to act on behalf of, to represent
港湾	gǎng wān	Noun: natural harbour, bay
迹象	jì xiàng	Noun: sign, indication
理智	lǐ zhì	Noun: reason, intellect
期限	qī xiàn	Noun: deadline, time limit
事态	shì tài	Noun: situation, state of affairs
误解	wù jiě	Noun: misunderstanding Verb: to misunderstand
隐约	yǐn yuē	Adjective: indistinct, faint
专长	zhuān cháng	Noun: specialty, special skill
执行	zhí xíng	Verb: to carry out, to execute
便于	biàn yú	Adjective: easy, convenient
带领	dài lǐng	Verb: to guide, to lead
岗位	gǎng wèi	Noun: post, position, station

记性	jì xing	Noun: memory, recall
立场	lì chǎng	Noun: position, standpoint, stand
奇妙	qí miào	Adjective: wonderful, fantastic
试图	shì tú	Verb: to attempt, to try
物美价廉	wù měi jià lián	Adjective: cheap and fine
专程	zhuān chéng	Noun: special-purpose trip
波涛	bō tāo	Noun: great wave, tidal wave
辩证	biàn zhèng	Adjective: dialectical, not good and not bad
怠慢	dài màn	Verb: to neglect, to slight
杠杆	gàng gǎn	Noun: lever
纪要	jì yào	Noun: minutes, written summary of a meeting
历代	lì dài	Time: through the ages, successive generations
旗袍	qí páo	Noun: Chinese dress
示威	shì wēi	Noun: demonstration Verb: to demonstrate against
婴儿	yīng ér	Noun: baby, infant
直径	zhí jìng	Noun: diameter
变质	biàn zhì	Noun: metamorphosis Verb: to go bad, to deteriorate
担保	dān bǎo	Verb: to assure, to guarantee, to vouch for
高超	gāo chāo	Adjective: excellent, outstanding, superb
记载	jì zǎi	Noun: record Verb: to write down
利害	lì hài	Noun: pros and cons
齐全	qí quán	Adjective: complete
事务	shì wù	Noun: work, routine, affair
物资	wù zī	Noun: goods and materials
英明	yīng míng	Adjective: wise, brilliant
专利	zhuān lì	Noun: patent
辫子	biàn zi	Noun: queue, plait, pigtail
胆怯	dǎn qiè	Adjective: timid, cowardly

高潮	gāo cháo	Noun: high tide, upsurge, climax, orgasm
家常	jiā cháng	Noun: daily life of a family
立交桥	lì jiāo qiáo	Noun: overpass, flyover
歧视	qí shì	Noun: discrimination Verb: to discriminate against
视线	shì xiàn	Noun: line of sight
溪	xī	Noun: small stream, small river
英勇	yīng yǒng	Noun: bravery Adjective: heroic, brave, valiant
专题	zhuān tí	Noun: special topic
标本	biāo běn	Noun: specimen, sample
蛋白质	dàn bái zhì	Noun: protein
高峰	gāo fēng	Noun: peak, summit
加工	jiā gōng	Noun: processing Verb: to process, to manufacture
历来	lì lái	Adverb: always, throughout the history
齐心协力	qí xīn xié lì	Verb: to work as one, to make concerted efforts
事项	shì xiàng	Noun: matter, item
膝盖	xī gài	Noun: knee
盈利	yíng lì	Noun: profit, gain
标记	biāo jì	Noun: sign, mark Verb: to mark up
诞辰	dàn chén	Noun: birthday
家伙	jiā huo	Noun: fellow, guy, tool, weapon
旗帜	qí zhì	Noun: flag, banner
试验	shì yàn	Noun: experiment Verb: to test, to experiment
熄灭	xī miè	Verb: to go out, to die out, to stop burning
迎面	yíng miàn	Adverb: head-on, face to face
转达	zhuǎn dá	Verb: to pass on, to convey, to communicate
淡季	dàn jì	Noun: off season
高明	gāo míng	Adjective: wise, brilliant, bright

加剧	jiā jù	Verb: to intensify, to sharpen, to aggravate
力所能及	lì suǒ néng jí	Verb: to be within one's power
起草	qǐ cǎo	Noun: draft Verb: to draft, to draw up
视野	shì yě	Noun: field of vision
转让	zhuǎn ràng	Verb: to transfer, to make over
居民	jū mín	Noun: resident
标题	biāo tí	Noun: title, heading, caption
诞生	dàn shēng	Verb: to be born, to be founded
高尚	gāo shàng	Adjective: nobly, lofty, sublime
家属	jiā shǔ	Noun: family member, dependent
立体	lì tǐ	Noun: solid Adjective: 3D, stereoscopic
启程	qǐ chéng	Verb: to set out on a journey
事业	shì yè	Noun: undertaking, career
昔日	xī rì	Time: formerly, in the old days
应酬	yìng chou	Noun: business dinner
转移	zhuǎn yí	Noun: metastasis Verb: to shift, to divert, to transfer
表决	biǎo jué	Verb: to decide by vote, to vote
淡水	dàn shuǐ	Noun: fresh water, potable water
高涨	gāo zhǎng	Noun: upsurge, wave Verb: to run high, to rise
佳肴	jiā yáo	Noun: delicacies, delicious food
起初	qǐ chū	Adverb: originally, at first
适宜	shì yí	Adjective: suitable, appropriate
牺牲	xī shēng	Noun: sacrifice Verb: to sacrifice oneself, to lay down one's life
应邀	yìng yāo	Adverb: on invitation, at sbd.'s invitation
转折	zhuǎn zhé	Noun: turn Verb: to turn in the course of an event
表态	biǎo tài	Verb: to declare one's position

当场	dāng chǎng	Adverb: on the spot, at the scene
稿件	gǎo jiàn	Noun: manuscript, rough draft
家喻户晓	jiā yù hù xiǎo	Adjective: widely known
例外	lì wài	Noun: exception Verb: to make an exception Adjective: exceptional
起伏	qǐ fú	Verb: to undulate, to move up and down
示意	shì yì	Noun: hint, sign, signal Verb: to hint, to signify
夕阳	xī yáng	Noun: the setting sun
拥护	yōng hù	Noun: advocacy Verb: to support, to stand up for, to advocate
传记	zhuàn jì	Noun: biography
液体	yè tǐ	Noun: liquid
表彰	biǎo zhāng	Verb: to commend, to honour
当初	dāng chū	Adverb: in the first place, originally
告辞	gào cí	Verb: to take leave, to bid farewell
夹杂	jiā zá	Verb: to be mixed up with, to be mingled with
力争	lì zhēng	Verb: to work hard for, to do all one can, to strive for, to argue strongly
乞丐	qǐ gài	Noun: beggar
收藏	shōu cáng	Verb: to collect, to store up
媳妇	xí fu	Noun: wife, daughter-in-law
庸俗	yōng sú	Adjective: vulgar, philistine
装备	zhuāng bèi	Noun: equipment Verb: to equip, to outfit
憋	biē	Verb: to hold back, to restrain, to suppress feelings
当面	dāng miàn	Adverb: face to face, in sbd.'s presence
告诫	gào jiè	Noun: warning, admonition Verb: to warn, to admonish
立足	lì zú	Verb: to have a footing, to base oneself on
起哄	qǐ hòng	Verb: to create a disturbance
收缩	shōu suō	Verb: to shrink, to contract

袭击	xí jī	Noun: surprise attack Verb: to attack by surprise, to raid
拥有	yōng yǒu	Verb: to have, to possess
装卸	zhuāng xiè	Verb: to load or unload, to assemble or disassemble
蜡烛	là zhú	Noun: candle
别墅	bié shù	Noun: villa
当前	dāng qián	Time: current, present
割	gē	Verb: to cut, to cut apart
联欢	lián huān	Verb: to have a get-together
起码	qǐ mǎ	Adverb: at the minimum, at least
收益	shōu yì	Noun: profit, income
习俗	xí sú	Noun: custom, tradition
永恒	yǒng héng	Noun: eternity Adjective: eternal, everlasting
庄严	zhuāng yán	Adjective: solemn, dignified, stately
别致	bié zhì	Adjective: unusual, unconventional, original
当事人	dāng shì rén	Noun: people concerned, party, client
搁	gē	Verb: to place, to put, to put aside
坚定	jiān dìng	Verb: to steady, to strengthen Adjective: firm, steady, staunch
廉洁	lián jié	Noun: integrity Adjective: honest, incorruptible
启示	qǐ shì	Noun: enlightenment, announcement, apocalypse
收音机	shōu yīn jī	Noun: radio
喜闻乐见	xǐ wén lè jiàn	Verb: to love to see and hear, a delight to see
涌现	yǒng xiàn	Verb: to emerge in large numbers, to spring up
庄重	zhuāng zhòng	Adjective: serious, grave, solemn
别扭	biè niu	Adjective: awkward (speech), difficult (personality), uncomfortable
当务之急	dāng wù zhī jí	Noun: matter of vital importance
疙瘩	gē da	Noun: lump, pimple, spot

监督	jiān dū	Noun: supervisor Verb: to control, to supervise
联络	lián luò	Noun: communication, connection Verb: to contact, to get in touch with
启事	qǐ shì	Noun: announcement, notice
手法	shǒu fǎ	Noun: technique, trick, skill
喜悦	xǐ yuè	Noun: joy, delight Adjective: happy, joyous
勇于	yǒng yú	Verb: to dare to, to have the courage to
幢	zhuàng	Measure Word: for houses, buildings, etc.
濒临	bīn lín	Adverb: on the verge of, close to
歌颂	gē sòng	Verb: to sing the praise of, to extol
尖端	jiān duān	Noun: sharp pointed end, tip, highest point, peak
联盟	lián méng	Noun: alliance, union, coalition
守护	shǒu hù	Verb: to guard, to protect
细胞	xì bāo	Noun: cell (biology)
踊跃	yǒng yuè	Verb: to leap, to jump Adjective: enthusiastic, eager
壮观	zhuàng guān	Adjective: spectacular, magnificent, imposing, grand
冰雹	bīng báo	Noun: hail
当选	dāng xuǎn	Verb: to be elected, to win an election
隔阂	gé hé	Noun: estrangement, barrier
坚固	jiān gù	Adjective: solid, firm, stable, strong
连年	lián nián	Adverb: for a series of years, over many years
岂有此理	qǐ yǒu cǐ lǐ	Adjective: outrageous, preposterous Expression: This is not true, is it?
手势	shǒu shì	Noun: gesture, sign, signal
细菌	xì jūn	Noun: bacterium, germ
壮丽	zhuàng lì	Noun: magnificence Adjective: magnificent, majestic, glorious
党	dǎng	Noun: party, association, society
格局	gé jú	Noun: layout, structure, pattern

艰难	jiān nán	Noun: difficulty, hardship Adjective: difficult, hard
连锁	lián suǒ	Noun: chain
起源	qǐ yuán	Noun: origin, source Verb: to originate, to come from
首要	shǒu yào	Adjective: most important, chief, principal
系列	xì liè	Noun: series
用户	yòng hù	Noun: user, consumer
壮烈	zhuàng liè	Adjective: brave, heroic
并非	bìng fēi	Adverb: really not, not so
档案	dàng àn	Noun: file, record, archive
隔离	gé lí	Verb: to separate, to isolate
坚韧	jiān rèn	Adjective: tough, durable, tenacious
连同	lián tóng	Relative Clause: together with, along with
器材	qì cái	Noun: equipment, material
手艺	shǒu yì	Noun: craftsmanship, handicraft
细致	xì zhì	Adjective: careful, fine, meticulous
优胜劣汰	yōu shèng liè tài	Noun: survival of the fittest
追悼	zhuī dào	Verb: to grieve for, to pay the last tribute to
并列	bìng liè	Verb: to stand side by side, to be juxtaposed
档次	dàng cì	Noun: grade, quality, level
格式	gé shi	Noun: format, specification
坚实	jiān shí	Adjective: solid, firm, substantial
联想	lián xiǎng	Noun: association Verb: to associate with sth.
气概	qì gài	Noun: mettle, spirit, lofty quality
授予	shòu yǔ	Verb: to award, to confer, to grant
霞	xiá	Noun: evening or morning glow
优先	yōu xiān	Noun: priority Adjective: preferential
追究	zhuī jiū	Verb: to investigate, to look into

倒闭	dǎo bì	Verb: to go bankrupt
各抒己见	gè shū jǐ jiàn	Verb: everyone gives their own view
监视	jiān shì	Verb: to monitor, to oversee, to watch
良心	liáng xīn	Noun: conscience
气功	qì gōng	Noun: Qigong
受罪	shòu zuì	Verb: to endure, to suffer, to have a hard time
狭隘	xiá ài	Adjective: narrow, tight, narrow minded
优异	yōu yì	Adjective: exceptional, outstanding
准则	zhǔn zé	Noun: norm, standard, criterion
汹涌	xiōng yǒng	Adjective: turbulent (ocean, sea, etc.)
革命	gé mìng	Noun: revolution
导弹	dǎo dàn	Noun: guided missile
个体	gè tǐ	Noun: individual, individuality Adjective: individual
坚硬	jiān yìng	Adjective: hard, solid
晾	liàng	Verb: to dry in the air
器官	qì guān	Noun: organ, apparatus
舒畅	shū chàng	Adjective: happy, entirely free from worry
峡谷	xiá gǔ	Noun: canyon, ravine
忧郁	yōu yù	Adjective: sullen, heavyhearted, melancholy
琢磨	zhuó mó	Verb: to ponder, to carve and polish
种植	zhòng zhí	Verb: to grow, to plant
波浪	bō làng	Noun: wave
导航	dǎo háng	Noun: navigation Verb: to navigate
跟前	gēn qián	Location: in front of
监狱	jiān yù	Noun: prison, jail
谅解	liàng jiě	Verb: understanding (sbd.)
迄今为止	qì jīn wéi zhǐ	Adverb: so far, up to now
书法	shū fǎ	Noun: calligraphy

狭窄	xiá zhǎi	Adjective: narrow, restricted (knowledge)
优越	yōu yuè	Noun: superiority Adjective: superior, advantageous
着手	zhuó shǒu	Verb: to set out, to start, to put one's hand to it
捣乱	dǎo luàn	Verb: to make trouble, to disturb
根深蒂固	gēn shēn dì gù	Adjective: deep-rooted, ineradicable
辽阔	liáo kuò	Adjective: vast, extensive
气魄	qì pò	Noun: daring, boldness, verve
疏忽	shū hu	Noun: negligence, carelessness Verb: to neglect, to omit
油腻	yóu nì	Adjective: oily, greasy
着想	zhuó xiǎng	Verb: to consider (other people's needs)
剥削	bō xuē	Noun: exploitation Verb: to exploit
导向	dǎo xiàng	Noun: guide, guideline
跟随	gēn suí	Verb: to follow
拣	jiǎn	Verb: to choose, to pick
列举	liè jǔ	Noun: list Verb: to list, to enumerate
气色	qì sè	Noun: complexion, colour
书籍	shū jí	Noun: books, works, literature
下属	xià shǔ	Noun: subordinate, vassal
油漆	yóu qī	Noun: oil paints, lacquer Verb: to paint
卓越	zhuó yuè	Adjective: excellent, outstanding, distinguished
当代	dāng dài	Time: present, nowadays
播种	bō zhòng	Noun: seed Verb: to sow
根源	gēn yuán	Noun: origin, root, source
剪彩	jiǎn cǎi	Verb: to cut the ribbon (at opening ceremony)
淋	lín	Verb: to sprinkle, to drench, to filter
气势	qì shì	Noun: momentum, vigor, imposing manner

书记	shū jì	Noun: secretary
先进	xiān jìn	Adjective: advanced, developed
犹如	yóu rú	Adverb: similar to, as if, just like
着重	zhuó zhòng	Verb: to stress, to put emphasis on
鸽子	gē zi	Noun: pigeon
博大精深	bó dà jīng shēn	Adjective: wide-ranging and profound
稻谷	dào gǔ	Noun: paddy, rice crops
跟踪	gēn zōng	Verb: to tail, to run after, to follow
简化	jiǎn huà	Verb: to simplify
临床	lín chuáng	Adjective: clinical
气味	qì wèi	Noun: odour, scent
书面	shū miàn	Adjective: written, in written form
鲜明	xiān míng	Adjective: clear-cut, distinct, colourful
有条不紊	yǒu tiáo bù wěn	Adjective: methodically, in an orderly way
资本	zī běn	Noun: capital
维护	wéi hù	Verb: to defend, to safeguard, to maintain
搏斗	bó dòu	Noun: combat, fight Verb: to fight, to struggle, to wrestle
盗窃	dào qiè	Noun: steal Verb: to steal
耕地	gēng dì	Noun: arable land, cultivated land
简陋	jiǎn lòu	Adjective: simple and crude
吝啬	lìn sè	Adjective: stingy, mean, miserly
气象	qì xiàng	Noun: meteorology
掀起	xiān qǐ	Verb: to lift, to begin, to set off
诱惑	yòu huò	Noun: temptation, enticement Verb: to entice, to lure, to tempt
资产	zī chǎn	Noun: property, assets
博览会	bó lǎn huì	Noun: exhibition, international fair
得不偿失	dé bù cháng shī	Verb: the game is not worth the candle
更新	gēng xīn	Verb: to replace, to renew, to update

检讨	jiǎn tǎo	Noun: self-criticism
凌晨	líng chén	Time: early in the morning
气压	qì yā	Noun: atmospheric pressure
竖	shù	Verb: to erect, to stand Adjective: vertical
先前	xiān qián	Adverb: before, previously
幼稚	yòu zhì	Adjective: childish, immature, naive
资深	zī shēn	Adjective: senior, deeply qualified
砖	zhuān	Noun: brick
伯母	bó mǔ	Noun: aunt (wife of father's elder brother)
得力	dé lì	Adjective: capable, competent
更正	gēng zhèng	Noun: correction Verb: to correct, to make a correction
简体字	jiǎn tǐ zì	Noun: simplified character
灵感	líng gǎn	Noun: inspiration, insight
掐	qiā	Verb: to pick, to pinch, to clutch
束	shù	Noun: bundle, cluster Verb: to bind, to tie Measure Word: for a bundle of
纤维	xiān wéi	Noun: fibre
愚蠢	yú chǔn	Adjective: stupid, foolish, silly
姿态	zī tài	Noun: posture, gesture, attitude, bearing
薄弱	bó ruò	Adjective: weak, frail
得天独厚	dé tiān dú hòu	Adjective: blessed, gifted, rich, unique, advantageous
公安局	gōng ān jú	Noun: Public Security Bureau
检验	jiǎn yàn	Noun: test Verb: to examine, to check, to test, to inspect
灵魂	líng hún	Noun: soul, spirit
恰当	qià dàng	Adjective: suitable, appropriate, proper
数额	shù é	Noun: amount
弦	xián	Noun: bowstring, string, hypotenuse

舆论	yú lùn	Noun: public opinion
滋味	zī wèi	Noun: taste, flavour
补偿	bǔ cháng	Noun: compensation Verb: to compensate, to make up
得罪	dé zuì	Verb: to offend, to displease, to commit an offense
供不应求	gōng bú yìng qiú	Verb: supply does not meet demand
简要	jiǎn yào	Adjective: concise, brief
伶俐	líng lì	Adjective: clever, smart, witty
恰到好处	qià dào hǎo chù	Adjective: just right
束缚	shù fù	Noun: constraint, shackles Verb: to restrict, to bind, to tie down
嫌	xián	Noun: suspicion, resentment Verb: to dislike, to mind
愚昧	yú mèi	Noun: ignorance Adjective: ignorant, fatuous
补救	bǔ jiù	Verb: to remedy, to redeem
蹬	dēng	Verb: to tread on, to step on
公道	gōng dao	Noun: justice Adjective: fair, just
溅	jiàn	Verb: to splash, to spatter
灵敏	líng mǐn	Adjective: smart, sensitive, keen
恰巧	qià qiǎo	Adverb: fortunately, by chance
树立	shù lì	Verb: to set up, to establish
闲话	xián huà	Noun: gossip, digression
渔民	yú mín	Noun: fisherman
资助	zī zhù	Noun: support, patronage Verb: to sponsor, to subsidize, to give financial assistance
哺乳	bǔ rǔ	Verb: to suckle, to breast-feed
灯笼	dēng long	Noun: lantern
宫殿	gōng diàn	Noun: palace
鉴别	jiàn bié	Verb: to differentiate, to distinguish
零星	líng xīng	Adjective: fragmentary, scattered, sporadic

洽谈	qià tán	Verb: to talk over with, to negotiate with
贤惠	xián huì	Adjective: chaste, virtuous (woman)
与日俱增	yǔ rì jù zēng	Verb: to increase steadily
子弹	zǐ dàn	Noun: bullet, cartridge
品种	pǐn zhǒng	Noun: variety, breed
补贴	bǔ tiē	Noun: subsidy, allowance
登陆	dēng lù	Verb: to land, to disembark, to log in
间谍	jiàn dié	Noun: spy
领会	lǐng huì	Verb: to understand, to grasp
牵扯	qiān chě	Verb: to implicate, to involve
耍	shuǎ	Verb: to play with
衔接	xián jiē	Verb: to join together, to combine
羽绒服	yǔ róng fú	Noun: down jacket
自卑	zì bēi	Verb: to feel inferior, to abase oneself
委托	wěi tuō	Verb: to entrust, to commission, to consign
捕捉	bǔ zhuō	Verb: to catch
登录	dēng lù	Verb: to register, to login
公告	gōng gào	Noun: announcement, bulletin
鉴定	jiàn dìng	Noun: evaluation Verb: to appraise, to evaluate
领事馆	lǐng shì guǎn	Noun: consulate
衰老	shuāi lǎo	Verb: to age, to grow old Adjective: old and weak
嫌疑	xián yí	Noun: suspicion
自发	zì fā	Adjective: spontaneous
嘱咐	zhǔ fù	Verb: to exhort, to enjoin, to tell
不得已	bù dé yǐ	Verb: to have no alternative but to
等级	děng jí	Noun: grade, rank
公关	gōng guān	Noun: public relations
见多识广	jiàn duō shí guǎng	Adjective: experienced and knowledgeable

领土	lǐng tǔ	Noun: territory
千方百计	qiān fāng bǎi jì	Verb: to try every possible way
衰退	shuāi tuì	Noun: recession, decline Verb: to decline, to fall
显著	xiǎn zhù	Adjective: notable, outstanding, remarkable
愈	yù	Verb: to recover Conjunction: the more ... the more
自力更生	zì lì gēng shēng	Verb: to rely on your strengths, to be self-reliant
步伐	bù fá	Noun: pace, step, march
瞪	dèng	Verb: to stare, to open (one's eyes)
攻击	gōng jī	Noun: attack Verb: to attack, to accuse
间隔	jiàn gé	Noun: interval, gap, compartment
领悟	lǐng wù	Verb: to understand, to comprehend
迁就	qiān jiù	Verb: to accommodate to, to yield, to meet halfway
率领	shuài lǐng	Verb: to lead, to command
现场	xiàn chǎng	Noun: scene, site, locale Adjective: live, on-the-spot, on-site
熨	yùn	Verb: to iron
自满	zì mǎn	Adjective: complacent, self-satisfied
不妨	bù fáng	Adverb: might as well
供给	gōng jǐ	Verb: to supply, to furnish, to provide
间接	jiàn jiē	Adjective: indirect
领先	lǐng xiān	Verb: to lead, to be in front
签署	qiān shǔ	Verb: to sign
涮火锅	shuàn huǒ guō	Verb: to eat hot pot
现成	xiàn chéng	Adjective: ready-made, readily available
预料	yù liào	Verb: to anticipate, to predict, to expect
不敢当	bù gǎn dāng	Expression: You flatter me!
敌视	dí shì	Verb: to be hostile to, to stand against
恭敬	gōng jìng	Adjective: deferential, respectful

见解	jiàn jiě	Noun: opinion, view, understanding
领袖	lǐng xiù	Noun: leader
迁徙	qiān xǐ	Verb: to move, to migrate
双胞胎	shuāng bāo tāi	Noun: twins
宪法	xiàn fǎ	Noun: constitution (law)
预期	yù qī	Verb: to expect, to anticipate Adjective: expected
自主	zì zhǔ	Noun: autonomy, independence Verb: to decide for oneself
布告	bù gào	Noun: notice, bulletin Verb: to announce
抵达	dǐ dá	Verb: to arrive, to reach
健全	jiàn quán	Adjective: healthy, strong, robust
溜	liū	Verb: to skate, to escape in stealth, to sneak off
谦逊	qiān xùn	Noun: modesty, humility Adjective: modest, humble
爽快	shuǎng kuài	Adjective: refreshed, rejuvenated, frank, outright
陷害	xiàn hài	Verb: to frame up
踪迹	zōng jì	Noun: trail, trace, footprint
不顾	bú gù	Verb: to ignore, to disregard Adverb: in spite of, regardless of
抵抗	dǐ kàng	Noun: resistance Verb: to resist, to fight back
攻克	gōng kè	Verb: to capture, to take, to seize
践踏	jiàn tà	Verb: to trample, to tread on
流浪	liú làng	Noun: vagrant life Verb: to roam about, to wander, to be homeless
牵制	qiān zhì	Verb: to curb, to pin down, to control
水利	shuǐ lì	Noun: water conservancy, irrigation works
馅儿	xiàn r	Noun: filling
预算	yù suàn	Noun: budget
棕色	zōng sè	Adjective: brown

不禁	bù jīn	Adverb: can't help, can't refrain from
抵制	dǐ zhì	Verb: to boycott, to resist, to reject
功劳	gōng láo	Noun: contribution, credit, meritorious service
舰艇	jiàn tǐng	Noun: warship, naval vessel
留恋	liú liàn	Verb: to be reluctant to leave, to recall with nostalgia
前景	qián jǐng	Noun: prospect, perspective, foreground
水龙头	shuǐ lóng tóu	Noun: faucet, tap
陷入	xiàn rù	Verb: to get caught up in, to sink into
欲望	yù wàng	Noun: desire, longing, appetite
宗旨	zōng zhǐ	Noun: objective, aim, purpose
粒	lì	Noun: grain Measure Word: for small round things
布局	bù jú	Noun: arrangement, composition
地步	dì bù	Noun: tight condition, plight, extent
公民	gōng mín	Noun: citizen
见闻	jiàn wén	Noun: what one sees and hears, knowledge, experience
流露	liú lù	Verb: to express, to reveal (feelings)
潜力	qián lì	Noun: potential, capacity
水泥	shuǐ ní	Noun: cement
线索	xiàn suǒ	Noun: clue, hint, trail
预先	yù xiān	Adverb: beforehand, prior
总而言之	zǒng ér yán zhī	Adverb: in short, in a word
丙	bǐng	Number: third(ly)
不堪	bù kān	Verb: can't bear, can't stand Adverb: utterly, extremely
地势	dì shì	Noun: topography, terrain
见义勇为	jiàn yì yǒng wéi	Verb: to stand up bravely for the truth
流氓	liú máng	Noun: hooligan, hoodlum, gangster
潜水	qián shuǐ	Noun: diving Verb: to dive, to go under water

司法	sī fǎ	Noun: judicature, justice
现状	xiàn zhuàng	Noun: current situation, status quo
预言	yù yán	Noun: prophecy Verb: to predict
总和	zǒng hé	Noun: sum
不可思议	bù kě sī yì	Expression: unbelievable!
递增	dì zēng	Noun: to increase progressively
公然	gōng rán	Adjective: flagrantly, undisguised
鉴于	jiàn yú	Pronoun: in view of, considering
留念	liú niàn	Verb: to keep as a souvenir
前提	qián tí	Noun: precondition, prerequisite
司令	sī lìng	Noun: commander, commanding officer
相差	xiāng chà	Verb: to differ
寓言	yù yán	Noun: fable
纵横	zòng héng	Adjective: with great ease, freely, vertically and horizontally
钙	gài	Noun: calcium
煎	jiān	Verb: to pan fry
不愧	bú kuì	Adverb: be worthy of, creditably
地质	dì zhì	Noun: geology
公认	gōng rèn	Verb: to be generally acknowledged
将近	jiāng jìn	Adverb: nearly, about, on the verge of
留神	liú shén	Verb: to take care, to watch out
潜移默化	qián yí mò huà	Verb: to influence secretly
思念	sī niàn	Verb: to miss, to think of, to long for
相等	xiāng děng	Verb: to be equal Adjective: equal
预兆	yù zhào	Noun: omen, portent
走廊	zǒu láng	Noun: corridor, aisle, piazza
立方	lì fāng	Noun: cube
不料	bú liào	Adverb: unexpectedly

颠簸	diān bǒ	Verb: to jolt, to bump
公式	gōng shì	Noun: formula
将军	jiāng jūn	Noun: admiral, general Verb: to challenge
流通	liú tōng	Noun: circulation Verb: to circulate, to flow
谴责	qiǎn zé	Noun: condemnation Verb: to denounce, to condemn, to criticize
思索	sī suǒ	Verb: to think deeply, to ponder
相辅相成	xiāng fǔ xiāng chéng	Verb: to complement each other
冤枉	yuān wang	Verb: to treat sbd. unjustly, to do sbd. wrong Adjective: not worth the effort, not worthwhile
走漏	zǒu lòu	Verb: to leak out, to divulge
不时	bù shí	Adverb: now and then, from time to time
颠倒	diān dǎo	Verb: to turn upside down Adjective: reversed, inverted, confused
公务	gōng wù	Noun: public affairs, official business
僵硬	jiāng yìng	Adjective: stiff, stark, inflexible
聋哑	lóng yǎ	Adjective: deaf and dumb
抢劫	qiǎng jié	Noun: robbery Verb: to rob, to plunder
思维	sī wéi	Noun: thought, thinking
镶嵌	xiāng qiàn	Noun: mosaic Verb: to inlay, to embed, to set
原告	yuán gào	Noun: plaintiff
走私	zǒu sī	Noun: smuggling Verb: to smuggle
实行	shí xíng	Verb: to put into practice, to carry out
部署	bù shǔ	Verb: to dispose, to deploy
典礼	diǎn lǐ	Noun: celebration, ceremony
功效	gōng xiào	Noun: efficacy
桨	jiǎng	Noun: oar, paddle
隆重	lóng zhòng	Adjective: ceremonious, solemn, grand

强制	qiáng zhì	Noun: enforcement Verb: to enforce, to compel
斯文	sī wen	Adjective: refined, educated, gentle
相应	xiāng yìng	Verb: to correspond Adjective: corresponding, appropriate, relevant
原理	yuán lǐ	Noun: principle, theory
揍	zòu	Verb: to beat up, to break to pieces
部位	bù wèi	Noun: position, place, section
典型	diǎn xíng	Noun: typical case, model
工艺品	gōng yì pǐn	Noun: handicraft
奖励	jiǎng lì	Noun: reward Verb: to reward
垄断	lǒng duàn	Noun: monopoly Verb: to monopolize
抢救	qiǎng jiù	Verb: to rescue, to save
乡镇	xiāng zhèn	Noun: village, township
园林	yuán lín	Noun: garden, park
租赁	zū lìn	Verb: to lease, to rent, to hire
不惜	bù xī	Verb: to not hesitate to
点缀	diǎn zhuì	Verb: to intersperse, to embellish, to decorate
公正	gōng zhèng	Noun: justice Adjective: just, fair
奖赏	jiǎng shǎng	Noun: reward, prize (money) Verb: to reward
笼罩	lǒng zhào	Verb: to envelop, to shroud
强迫	qiǎng pò	Verb: to compel, to force
私自	sī zì	Adverb: without approval, secretly, privately
想方设法	xiāng fāng shè fǎ	Verb: to do everything possible
圆满	yuán mǎn	Adjective: satisfactory, perfect
足以	zú yǐ	Adverb: enough to, sufficient to
喂	wèi	Verb: to feed, to breed
等候	děng hòu	Verb: to wait

不相上下	bù xiāng shàng xià	Adjective: about the same
垫	diàn	Noun: pad, cushion, mat Verb: to pad
公证	gōng zhèng	Noun: notarization Verb: to notarize
降临	jiàng lín	Verb: to befall, to arrive
搂	lǒu	Verb: to hug, to embrace
桥梁	qiáo liáng	Noun: bridge
死亡	sǐ wáng	Noun: death Verb: to die
响亮	xiǎng liàng	Adjective: loud and clear, resounding
源泉	yuán quán	Noun: source, fountain, spring
朴素	pǔ sù	Adjective: plain, simple
不像话	bú xiàng huà	Adjective: unreasonable, shocking, outrageous
奠定	diàn dìng	Verb: to establish, to found
巩固	gǒng gù	Noun: consolidation Verb: to consolidate, to solidify
交叉	jiāo chā	Verb: to cross, to intersect
炉灶	lú zào	Noun: stove
翘	qiào	Verb: to raise, to hold up Adjective: outstanding
肆无忌惮	sì wú jì dàn	Adjective: unrestrained, without the slightest scruple
响应	xiǎng yìng	Verb: to answer, to respond to
原始	yuán shǐ	Adjective: original, primitive, first-hand
阻碍	zǔ ài	Verb: to obstruct, to hinder, to block
不屑一顾	bú xiè yí gù	Verb: to disdain as beneath contempt
惦记	diàn jì	Verb: to be concerned about, keep thinking about
共和国	gòng hé guó	Noun: republic
交代	jiāo dài	Verb: to explain, to justify oneself, to hand over (duties), to confess
轮船	lún chuán	Noun: steamship
锲而不舍	qiè ér bù shě	Verb: to keep on working with perseverance

饲养	sì yǎng	Verb: to raise, to rear
巷	xiàng	Noun: lane, alley
元首	yuán shǒu	Noun: head of state
祖父	zǔ fù	Noun: grandfather (paternal)
不言而喻	bù yán ér yù	Verb: to go without saying, to be self-evident
电源	diàn yuán	Noun: electric power source
共计	gòng jì	Noun: total Verb: to total, to count up
焦点	jiāo diǎn	Noun: focus, focal point
轮廓	lún kuò	Noun: outline, contour, silhouette
切实	qiè shí	Adjective: feasible, realistic, practical
四肢	sì zhī	Noun: arms and legs, four limbs
元素	yuán sù	Noun: element, basic element
阻拦	zǔ lán	Verb: to stop, to obstruct
不由得	bù yóu de	Adverb: can't help, cannot but
叼	diāo	Verb: to hold by the teeth or lips
共鸣	gòng míng	Noun: resonance, sympathy
焦急	jiāo jí	Noun: anxiety Adjective: anxious, worried
轮胎	lún tāi	Noun: tire
侵犯	qīn fàn	Verb: to infringe on, to violate (law, rule, etc.)
耸	sǒng	Verb: to shrug, to startle
向导	xiàng dǎo	Noun: guide
原先	yuán xiān	Adjective: former, original
阻挠	zǔ náo	Verb: to thwart, to obstruct
不择手段	bù zé shǒu duàn	Expression: by hook or by crook
雕刻	diāo kè	Noun: carving Verb: to carve, to engrave
勾结	gōu jié	Verb: to collude with, to gang up with
娇气	jiāo qì	Adjective: squeamish, finicky
论坛	lùn tán	Noun: forum (for discussion)

钦佩	qīn pèi	Verb: to admire, to look up to
艘	sōu	Measure Word: for ships, boats
向来	xiàng lái	Adverb: always, all along
元宵节	Yuán xiāo jié	Noun: Lantern festival
钻研	zuān yán	Verb: to study in depth, to dig into
不止	bù zhǐ	Adverb: without end, more than, not limited to
雕塑	diāo sù	Noun: statue, sculpture Verb: to carve
钩子	gōu zi	Noun: hook
交涉	jiāo shè	Verb: to negotiate
论证	lùn zhèng	Noun: proof Verb: to prove a point, to expound on
亲热	qīn rè	Adjective: intimate, loving, affectionate
向往	xiàng wǎng	Verb: to yearn for, to look forward to
约束	yuē shù	Noun: restriction, constraint Verb: to restrict, to limit to
钻石	zuàn shí	Noun: diamond
布置	bù zhì	Verb: to fix up, to arrange, to decorate
吊	diào	Verb: to hang, to suspend, to express condolence to
构思	gòu sī	Noun: conception Verb: to design, to conceive
啰唆	luō suo	Verb: to grumble
苏醒	sū xǐng	Verb: to wake up, to regain consciousness
消除	xiāo chú	Verb: to eliminate, to remove
嘴唇	zuǐ chún	Noun: lip
裁缝	cái feng	Noun: tailor Verb: to sew
调动	diào dòng	Verb: to transfer, to manoeuvre (troops, etc.)
孤独	gū dú	Adjective: lonely
交易	jiāo yì	Noun: transaction, business deal, trade
勤俭	qín jiǎn	Adjective: hardworking and frugal
俗话	sú huà	Noun: proverb, saying

消毒	xiāo dú	Noun: disinfection, sterilization Verb: to disinfect, to sterilize
乐谱	yuè pǔ	Noun: musical score, notation
遵循	zūn xún	Verb: to follow, to abide by
财富	cái fù	Noun: wealth, riches
跌	diē	Verb: to drop, to fall down
辜负	gū fù	Verb: to fail to live up to, to be unworthy of, to disappoint
搅拌	jiǎo bàn	Verb: to stir, to mix up
落成	luò chéng	Noun: completion of a building Verb: to complete (building)
消防	xiāo fáng	Noun: fire control, fire fighting
蕴藏	yùn cáng	Verb: to hold in store, to contain
尊严	zūn yán	Noun: dignity, honour
尖锐	jiān ruì	Adjective: sharp, acute (illness)
才干	cái gàn	Noun: ability, competence, talent
盯	dīng	Verb: to gaze at, fix one's eyes on, to watch attentively
孤立	gū lì	Noun: isolation Verb: to isolate Adjective: isolated
角落	jiǎo luò	Noun: corner, nook
落实	luò shí	Verb: to carry out, to implement Adjective: practical, workable
诉讼	sù sòng	Noun: lawsuit, litigation
消耗	xiāo hào	Noun: consumption Verb: to use up, to consume
酝酿	yùn niàng	Verb: to brew, to ferment, to incubate (used in abstract way)
散布	sàn bù	Verb: to scatter, to sow, to spread
裁判	cái pàn	Noun: judgment, referee, judge, umpire Verb: to act as referee
叮嘱	dīng zhǔ	Verb: to exhort repeatedly, to urge
姑且	gū qiě	Adverb: temporarily, for the moment
缴纳	jiǎo nà	Verb: to pay (taxes)

络绎不绝	luò yì bù jué	Adverb: continuously, in an endless stream
清澈	qīng chè	Adjective: clear, limpid
塑造	sù zào	Verb: to shape, to mould
销毁	xiāo huǐ	Verb: to destroy (by melting or burning)
运算	yùn suàn	Noun: operation (mathematical) Verb: to calculate
作弊	zuò bì	Verb: to cheat, to practice fraud
财务	cái wù	Noun: financial affairs
定期	dìng qī	Adjective: regular, periodical
股东	gǔ dōng	Noun: shareholder, stockholder
较量	jiào liàng	Verb: to have a contest, to compete
屡次	lǚ cì	Adverb: repeatedly
清晨	qīng chén	Time: early morning
素质	sù zhì	Noun: quality, basic essence
运行	yùn xíng	Verb: to be in motion, to run
裁员	cái yuán	Verb: to cut staff, to lay off employees
定义	dìng yì	Noun: definition
古董	gǔ dǒng	Noun: antique, curio
教养	jiào yǎng	Noun: upbringing, education Verb: to educate, to bring up
履行	lǚ xíng	Verb: to carry out, to fulfil
清除	qīng chú	Verb: to clear away, to eliminate, to get rid of
小心翼翼	xiǎo xīn yì yì	Adjective: very careful, prudent, deliberate
孕育	yùn yù	Noun: gestation Verb: to be pregnant, to gestate
作废	zuò fèi	Verb: to become invalid, to cancel, to delete
财政	cái zhèng	Noun: finance, public finances
丢人	diū rén	Verb: to lose face
鼓动	gǔ dòng	Verb: to agitate, to arouse, to incite
皆	jiē	Adverb: all, each and every
掠夺	lüè duó	Verb: to plunder, to rob

算数	suàn shù	Verb: to count, to hold, to keep one's word, to be valid
肖像	xiào xiàng	Noun: portrait
砸	zá	Verb: to smash, to pound, to fail
作风	zuò fēng	Noun: style, attitude, way of work
采购	cǎi gòu	Verb: to procure, to purchase
丢三落四	diū sān là sì	Adjective: forgetful, scatterbrained
股份	gǔ fèn	Noun: share, stock
阶层	jiē céng	Noun: hierarchy, social stratum
清洁	qīng jié	Adjective: clean, unpolluted
随即	suí jí	Adverb: immediately, right afterwards
效益	xiào yì	Noun: benefit
杂技	zá jì	Noun: acrobatics
作息	zuò xī	Verb: to work and rest
武器	wǔ qì	Noun: weapon, arms
采集	cǎi jí	Verb: to gather, to collect
东道主	dōng dào zhǔ	Noun: host
骨干	gǔ gàn	Noun: backbone, diaphysis
麻痹	má bì	Noun: paralysis Adjective: numb, lull
清理	qīng lǐ	Verb: to clean up, to put in order, to check up
携带	xié dài	Verb: to carry, to take along
杂交	zá jiāo	Noun: hybrid Verb: to hybridize, to cross
座右铭	zuò yòu míng	Noun: motto, maxim
采纳	cǎi nà	Verb: to accept, to adopt
东张西望	dōng zhāng xī wàng	Verb: to peer in all directions, to look around
古怪	gǔ guài	Adjective: eccentric, cranky, oddly, grotesque
接连	jiē lián	Adverb: in succession, in a row, one after another
麻木	má mù	Adjective: numb, insensitive

倾听	qīng tīng	Verb: to listen attentively, to give an ear to
协会	xié huì	Noun: association, union, society
咋	ză	Adverb: why, how
做主	zuò zhŭ	Verb: to decide, to take charge of, to support
不免	bù miăn	Adverb: inevitably
彩票	căi piào	Noun: lottery, lottery ticket
董事长	dŏng shì zhăng	Noun: chairman of the board, president
顾虑	gù lǜ	Noun: misgivings, apprehensions Verb: to have misgivings about
揭露	jiē lù	Noun: disclosure Verb: to expose, to unmask, to disclose
麻醉	má zuì	Noun: anaesthesia, narcosis Verb: to anesthetize
清晰	qīng xī	Adjective: clear, distinct
随意	suí yì	Adverb: as one wishes, voluntary, random
协商	xié shāng	Verb: to consult with, to talk things over, to negotiate about
灾难	zāi nàn	Noun: disaster, catastrophe
力求	lì qiú	Verb: to do one's best
企图	qĭ tú	Noun: attempt Verb: to attempt
参谋	cān móu	Noun: staff officer, advisor Verb: to give advice
栋	dòng	Measure Word: for houses, buildings
固然	gù rán	Adverb: admittedly, it is true, no doubt
杰出	jié chū	Adjective: outstanding, remarkable
码头	mă tóu	Noun: dock, pier, wharf
倾向	qīng xiàng	Noun: trend, tendency Verb: to tend to, to be inclined to
隧道	suì dào	Noun: tunnel
协议	xié yì	Noun: agreement, pact
栽培	zāi péi	Noun: cultivation, planting Verb: to grow, to cultivate

参照	cān zhào	Noun: reference Verb: to refer to, to consult
动荡	dòng dàng	Noun: turbulence, unrest (political), upheaval
顾问	gù wèn	Noun: adviser, consultant
竭尽全力	jié jìn quán lì	Verb: to spare no effort, to do all one can
嘛	ma	Particle: added to emphasize sth.
倾斜	qīng xié	Verb: to incline, to lean, to slant
岁月	suì yuè	Noun: years
协助	xié zhù	Verb: to assist, to help, to aid
宰	zǎi	Verb: to butcher, to slaughter
相声	xiàng shēng	Noun: cross-talk, comic dialogue
残酷	cán kù	Noun: cruelty Adjective: cruel, brutal
动机	dòng jī	Noun: motive, intention, motivation
故乡	gù xiāng	Noun: home, hometown
结晶	jié jīng	Noun: crystal, crystallization
埋伏	mái fú	Noun: ambush Verb: to ambush, to lurk
清醒	qīng xǐng	Adjective: clear-headed, sober, awake
损坏	sǔn huài	Verb: to damage, to break, to spoil
固体	gù tǐ	Noun: solid (body)
残留	cán liú	Verb: to remain, to be left over
冻结	dòng jié	Verb: to freeze (loan, price, etc.), to block
固有	gù yǒu	Adjective: intrinsic, inherent, native
结局	jié jú	Noun: ending, finale, conclusion
埋没	mái mò	Noun: oblivion Verb: to cover up (with earth, etc.), to bury
清真	qīng zhēn	Adjective: Muslim, halal (food)
屑	xiè	Noun: crumbs, filings Verb: to be worth it
再接再厉	zài jiē zài lì	Verb: to make persistent efforts, to double one's efforts
残忍	cán rěn	Adjective: cruel, merciless, brutal

动静	dòng jing	Noun: sound of movement, activity, happening
故障	gù zhàng	Noun: malfunction, breakdown, defect, fault
结算	jié suàn	Verb: to balance, to settle accounts
埋葬	mái zàng	Verb: to bury
情报	qíng bào	Noun: information, intelligence
索性	suǒ xìng	Adverb: might as well, simply
谢绝	xiè jué	Verb: to refuse politely
在意	zài yì	Verb: to care about, to take to heart
上进	shàng jìn	Verb: to make progress
削	xiāo	Verb: to peel, to sharpen, to cut (a ball)
灿烂	càn làn	Adjective: bright, splendid, brilliant
动力	dòng lì	Noun: power, driving force, motive power
固执	gù zhi	Adjective: stubborn, obstinate, pigheaded
截至	jié zhì	Relative Clause: up to, by (time)
迈	mài	Noun: mile Verb: to take a step, to stride
情节	qíng jié	Noun: story, plot, circumstances
塌	tā	Verb: to collapse, to fall down, to cave in
泄露	xiè lòu	Verb: to leak (information), to let out
攒	zǎn	Verb: to accumulate, to hoard, to save (money)
舱	cāng	Noun: cabin, hold
动脉	dòng mài	Noun: artery
拐杖	guǎi zhàng	Noun: walking stick, crutches
节奏	jié zòu	Noun: rhythm
脉搏	mài bó	Noun: pulse
晴朗	qíng lǎng	Noun: sunny, cloudless
踏实	tā shi	Adjective: down-to-earth, anxiety-free
泄气	xiè qì	Verb: to feel discouraged, to lose heart, to be frustrated
暂且	zàn qiě	Adverb: for now, for the moment, temporarily

雇佣	gù yōng	Verb: to employ, to hire
苍白	cāng bái	Adjective: pale, wan
动身	dòng shēn	Verb: to leave, to go on a journey
官方	guān fāng	Noun: officials, authorities Adjective: official, authoritative
解除	jiě chú	Noun: relief, dissolution Verb: to relief, to remove, to dissolve
埋怨	mán yuàn	Verb: to complain, to grumble
情理	qíng lǐ	Noun: reason, sense
台风	tái fēng	Noun: hurricane, typhoon
新陈代谢	xīn chén dài xiè	Noun: metabolism
赞叹	zàn tàn	Verb: to gasp in admiration, highly praise
晃	huàng	Verb: to sway
仓促	cāng cù	Adjective: hurried, hasty
动手	dòng shǒu	Verb: to start work, to begin, to hit with hands
观光	guān guāng	Noun: tourism, sightseeing Verb: to tour, to go sightseeing
解雇	jiě gù	Verb: to fire, to sack, to dismiss
漫长	màn cháng	Adjective: very long, endless
情形	qíng xíng	Noun: circumstances, situation
泰斗	tài dǒu	Noun: leading authority, magnate
心得	xīn dé	Noun: gained knowledge, what one has learned
仓库	cāng kù	Noun: storehouse, warehouse, depot
动态	dòng tài	Noun: developments, trends
关照	guān zhào	Verb: to take care, to look after, to inform
解剖	jiě pōu	Noun: dissection, anatomy Verb: to dissect, to anatomize
漫画	màn huà	Noun: caricature, cartoon, manga
请柬	qǐng jiǎn	Noun: invitation card
太空	tài kōng	Noun: outer space
新郎	xīn láng	Noun: bridegroom

牵	qiān	Verb: to pull, to lead, to hold hands
操劳	cāo láo	Verb: to work hard, to look after
管辖	guǎn xiá	Verb: to administer, to govern, to have jurisdiction over
解散	jiě sàn	Verb: to dissolve, to disband, to dismiss
慢性	màn xìng	Adjective: chronic
请教	qǐng jiào	Verb: to consult, seek advice
瘫痪	tān huàn	Noun: paralysis
心灵	xīn líng	Noun: heart, soul, spirit Adjective: bright, smart
赞助	zàn zhù	Noun: assistance, support Verb: to support, to assist, to sponsor
操练	cāo liàn	Noun: drill, exercise Verb: to drill, to practice
动员	dòng yuán	Noun: mobilization Verb: to mobilize, to arouse
罐	guàn	Noun: can, jar, pot
解体	jiě tǐ	Verb: to disintegrate
蔓延	màn yán	Verb: to extend, to spread, to creep
请示	qǐng shì	Verb: to ask for instructions
贪婪	tān lán	Noun: greed Adjective: greedy, avid, grasping
新娘	xīn niáng	Noun: bride
遭受	zāo shòu	Verb: to suffer, to be subject to
报警	bào jǐng	Verb: to sound an alarm, to report
操纵	cāo zòng	Verb: to operate, to control, to handle
兜	dōu	Noun: pocket, bag Verb: to wrap up (in clothes)
贯彻	guàn chè	Verb: to carry out, to implement, to put into practice
戒备	jiè bèi	Verb: to take precautions, to be on the alert
忙碌	máng lù	Adjective: busy
请帖	qǐng tiě	Noun: invitation card
辛勤	xīn qín	Adjective: industrious, hardworking, diligent

糟蹋	zāo tà	Verb: to waste, to wreck, to ruin, to spoil, to insult
鄙视	bǐ shì	Verb: to look down upon
操作	cāo zuò	Noun: operation, handling Verb: to work, to operate, to manipulate
陡峭	dǒu qiào	Adjective: steep, cliffy, precipitous
灌溉	guàn gài	Noun: irrigation Verb: to irrigate, to water
借鉴	jiè jiàn	Verb: to take example by, to use as reference
茫茫	máng máng	Adjective: boundless, vast
丘陵	qiū líng	Noun: hill
贪污	tān wū	Noun: corruption Adjective: corrupt
薪水	xīn shuǐ	Noun: salary, wage
遭殃	zāo yāng	Verb: to go through disaster, to suffer a calamity
编织	biān zhī	Verb: to weave, to knit
嘈杂	cáo zá	Adjective: noisy, rackety
斗争	dòu zhēng	Noun: struggle, fight Verb: to fight, to combat, to battle
惯例	guàn lì	Noun: convention, tradition
界限	jiè xiàn	Noun: boundary, limit, border
盲目	máng mù	Adjective: blind, aimless
区分	qū fēn	Verb: to distinguish, to differentiate between
弹性	tán xìng	Noun: elasticity
心态	xīn tài	Noun: attitude, way of thinking, mentality
遭遇	zāo yù	Verb: to meet with (sth. unfortunate), to encounter
插座	chā zuò	Noun: socket, (power) outlet
草案	cǎo àn	Noun: draft
督促	dū cù	Verb: to urge sbd. to do sth.
光彩	guāng cǎi	Noun: lustre, splendour, brilliance Adjective: honourable, glorious

借助	jiè zhù	Adverb: with the help of, drawing support from
茫然	máng rán	Adjective: absent (mind), blank, puzzled
屈服	qū fú	Verb: to submit, to surrender, to yield
坦白	tǎn bái	Noun: confession Verb: to confess, to admit Adjective: frank, candid
心疼	xīn téng	Verb: to love dearly, to feel distressed, to feel sorry
巢穴	cháo xué	Noun: nest, lair
草率	cǎo shuài	Adjective: careless, hasty, sloppy
光辉	guāng huī	Noun: radiance, brilliance Adjective: brilliant, magnificent
津津有味	jīn jīn yǒu wèi	Verb: to do with great pleasure, to relish
冒充	mào chōng	Verb: to feign, to pretend to be
区域	qū yù	Noun: area, region, district
探测	tàn cè	Noun: sounding, exploration Verb: to explore, to sound, to probe
欣慰	xīn wèi	Verb: to be gratified
造型	zào xíng	Noun: modelling, moulding Verb: to model, to mould
衬托	chèn tuō	Verb: to set off, make something seem nicer than it is
策划	cè huà	Verb: to plan, to plot, to engineer
独裁	dú cái	Noun: dictatorship, autocracy
光芒	guāng máng	Noun: rays of light
金融	jīn róng	Noun: finance, banking
茂盛	mào shèng	Adjective: luxuriant, exuberant, lush
曲折	qū zhé	Noun: complications, winding Adjective: complicated, winding, zigzag
叹气	tàn qì	Noun: sigh Verb: to sigh
欣欣向荣	xīn xīn xiàng róng	Adjective: flourishing, thriving
噪音	zào yīn	Noun: noise, rumble
迟钝	chí dùn	Adjective: sluggish

残疾	cán jí	Noun: disability, deformity Adjective: disabled, handicapped
丁	dīng	Number: fourth
测量	cè liáng	Verb: to measure, to survey
毒品	dú pǐn	Noun: drugs, narcotics, dope
广阔	guǎng kuò	Adjective: wide, vast
枚	méi	Measure Word: for medals, coins, rockets, etc.
驱逐	qū zhú	Verb: to expel, to banish
探索	tàn suǒ	Verb: to explore, to probe
心血	xīn xuè	Noun: painstaking effort, heart's blood
责怪	zé guài	Verb: to blame, to rebuke
炊烟	chuī yān	Expression: smoke in the kitchen (used in literature)
策略	cè lüè	Noun: tactics
赌博	dǔ bó	Noun: gambling Verb: to gamble, to bet
规范	guī fàn	Noun: norm, rule, standard
媒介	méi jiè	Noun: media, medium
渠道	qú dào	Noun: medium of communication, channel, ditch
探讨	tàn tǎo	Verb: to investigate, to discuss, to probe into
心眼儿	xīn yǎn r	Noun: mind, intention, cleverness
贼	zéi	Noun: thief
斑	bān	Noun: spot, stripe
慈善	cí shàn	Adjective: charitable
关怀	guān huái	Noun: care, solicitude Verb: to care for, to show solicitude for
宗教	zōng jiào	Noun: religion
侧面	cè miàn	Noun: side, flank, lateral
堵塞	dǔ sè	Noun: blockage Verb: to cause an obstruction, to stop
规格	guī gé	Noun: standard, norm, specification
取缔	qǔ dì	Verb: to ban, to prohibit

探望	tàn wàng	Verb: to visit
新颖	xīn yǐng	Adjective: new, original
增添	zēng tiān	Verb: to add, to increase
堤坝	dī bà	Noun: dam
层出不穷	céng chū bù qióng	Verb: to emerge in an endless stream
杜绝	dù jué	Verb: to put an end to, to eliminate
归根到底	guī gēn dào dǐ	Adverb: to sum it up, in a final analysis, in the long run
紧迫	jǐn pò	Adjective: urgent, pressing
曲子	qǔ zi	Noun: tune, melody, music
信赖	xìn lài	Verb: to trust, to rely on
赠送	zèng sòng	Verb: to present as a gift
方圆	fāng yuán	Noun: range, perimeter
层次	céng cì	Noun: arrangement of ideas, administrative level
端	duān	Noun: extremity, end, point Verb: to carry
规划	guī huà	Noun: plan, program Verb: to plan, to work out
美观	měi guān	Adjective: pleasing to the eye, beautiful, artistic
趣味	qù wèi	Noun: interest, delight, fun, taste
掏	tāo	Verb: to take out, to fish out
信念	xìn niàn	Noun: faith, belief, conviction
渣	zhā	Noun: dregs, sediment, residue
废寝忘食	fèi qǐn wàng shí	Expression: to be 100% focused on one thing and don't do anything else
端午节	Duān wǔ jié	Noun: Dragon Boat Festival
归还	guī huán	Verb: to return sth., to give back
进而	jìn ér	Conjunction: then, and then
美满	měi mǎn	Adjective: happy, blissful
圈套	quān tào	Noun: trap, snare
滔滔不绝	tāo tāo bù jué	Verb: talking non-stop

信仰	xìn yǎng	Noun: belief, conviction, faith Verb: to believe in
扎	zhā	Verb: to prick, to push a needle into
抚摸	fǔ mō	Verb: to fondle, to pet, to touch gently
查获	chá huò	Verb: to hunt down and seize
端正	duān zhèng	Adjective: upright, regular
进攻	jìn gōng	Verb: to attack, to assault
美妙	měi miào	Adjective: great, wonderful, beautiful, splendid
权衡	quán héng	Verb: to weigh, to balance, to consider
陶瓷	táo cí	Noun: ceramics, porcelain
信誉	xìn yù	Noun: prestige, reputation, standing
扎实	zhā shi	Adjective: strong, sturdy, robust
俯视	fǔ shì	Verb: to look down upon
岔	chà	Noun: fork in the road Verb: to diverge
短促	duǎn cù	Adjective: short, brief (time)
规章	guī zhāng	Noun: rule, regulation
进化	jìn huà	Noun: evolution
全局	quán jú	Noun: general situation
腥	xīng	Adjective: fishy (smell)
眨	zhǎ	Verb: to wink, to blink
呼唤	hū huàn	Verb: to shout (e.g. a name)
刹那	chà nà	Time: in an instant, split second
断定	duàn dìng	Verb: to conclude, to come to a judgement
轨道	guǐ dào	Noun: railway, track, orbit
近来	jìn lái	Adverb: recently, lately
全力以赴	quán lì yǐ fù	Verb: make an all-out effort, to go all out
淘汰	táo tài	Verb: to eliminate through selection, to wash
兴高采烈	xìng gāo cǎi liè	Verb: to be happy and excited, to be in high spirits

诈骗	zhà piàn	Verb: to defraud, to swindle
花蕾	huā lěi	Noun: flower bud
诧异	chà yì	Adjective: astonished, surprised
跪	guì	Verb: to kneel
浸泡	jìn pào	Verb: to soak, to immerse
萌芽	méng yá	Noun: sprout, germ, beginning (of sth.)
拳头	quán tou	Noun: fist
兴隆	xīng lóng	Adjective: prosperous, thriving
摘要	zhāi yào	Noun: summary, brief
荤	hūn	Noun: non-vegetarian food
柴油	chái yóu	Noun: diesel fuel
断绝	duàn jué	Verb: to sever, to break off
贵族	guì zú	Noun: nobleman, aristocrat, aristocracy, lord
晋升	jìn shēng	Verb: to promote (job)
猛烈	měng liè	Adjective: fierce, violent
权威	quán wēi	Noun: authority Adjective: authoritative
特长	tè cháng	Noun: personal strength, speciality
兴旺	xīng wàng	Adjective: prosperous, thriving
债券	zhài quàn	Noun: bond, debenture
剑	jiàn	Noun: sword
搀	chān	Verb: to assist by the arm, to support, to mix
堆积	duī jī	Verb: to pile up, to accumulate
棍棒	gùn bàng	Noun: club, cane, stick
特定	tè dìng	Adjective: special, specific, particular
刑事	xíng shì	Adjective: criminal, penal
沾光	zhān guāng	Verb: to benefit from association with sbd.
将就	jiāng jiu	Verb: to put up with, to accept
祖国	zǔ guó	Noun: fatherland, homeland

馋	chán	Adjective: greedy, gluttonous
对策	duì cè	Noun: countermeasure
国防	guó fáng	Noun: national defence
眯	mī	Verb: to narrow one's eyes, to take a nap
犬	quǎn	Noun: dog
形态	xíng tài	Noun: shape, form, pattern
瞻仰	zhān yǎng	Verb: look at with reverence
侥幸	jiǎo xìng	Noun: luck
缠绕	chán rào	Verb: to twine, to wind, to bother
对称	duì chèn	Noun: symmetry Adjective: symmetrical
国务院	guó wù yuàn	Noun: State Council (China), State Department (USA)
进展	jìn zhǎn	Noun: progress Verb: to evolve, to make progress
弥补	mí bǔ	Verb: to make up for, to compensate
缺口	quē kǒu	Noun: nick, jag, gap
提拔	tí bá	Verb: to select for promotion
行政	xíng zhèng	Noun: administration
斩钉截铁	zhǎn dīng jié tiě	Verb: to be resolute and decisive
节制	jié zhì	Noun: moderation Verb: to restrict, to control
勤劳	qín láo	Adjective: hardworking, industrious
祖先	zǔ xiān	Noun: ancestor
阐述	chǎn shù	Verb: to expound
对付	duì fu	Verb: to deal with, to cope with
果断	guǒ duàn	Adjective: firm, decisive
茎	jīng	Noun: stalk, stem
迷惑	mí huò	Verb: to puzzle, to confuse
缺席	quē xí	Noun: absence Adjective: absent
题材	tí cái	Noun: subject matter, theme

性感	xìng gǎn	Noun: sex appeal Adjective: sexy
展示	zhǎn shì	Noun: show, exhibition, demonstration Verb: to show, to reveal, to display
锦上添花	jǐn shàng tiān huā	Expression: to make something great even better
侵略	qīn lüè	Noun: invasion, aggression Verb: to invade
产业	chǎn yè	Noun: industry, property Adjective: industrial
过度	guò dù	Adjective: excessive
精打细算	jīng dǎ xì suàn	Noun: careful calculation and strict budgeting
弥漫	mí màn	Verb: to pervade, to fill the air with
缺陷	quē xiàn	Noun: defect, flaw
提炼	tí liàn	Verb: to extract, to refine
展望	zhǎn wàng	Noun: outlook, prospect Verb: to look ahead
敬业	jìng yè	Verb: to be dedicated to one's work
颤抖	chàn dǒu	Verb: to shudder, to shiver
对抗	duì kàng	Noun: resistance, confrontation Verb: to withstand, to resist
过渡	guò dù	Noun: transition Verb: to cross over Adjective: interim
惊动	jīng dòng	Verb: to disturb, to alert, to alarm
迷人	mí rén	Adjective: charming, fascinating
瘸	qué	Verb: to be lame, to limp
提示	tí shì	Verb: to prompt, to point out
性命	xìng mìng	Noun: life
展现	zhǎn xiàn	Verb: to unfold, to emerge, to come out
倔强	jué jiàng	Adjective: obstinate, stubborn
差别	chā bié	Noun: difference
对立	duì lì	Verb: to oppose Adjective: opposite, opposing
过奖	guò jiǎng	Verb: to overpraise, to flatter

经费	jīng fèi	Noun: expenditure, regular expenses, funds
确保	què bǎo	Verb: to assure, to guarantee
提议	tí yì	Noun: proposal, suggestion Verb: to propose, to suggest
性能	xìng néng	Noun: function, capability, performance
崭新	zhǎn xīn	Adjective: brand new
君子	jūn zǐ	Noun: nobleman, gentleman
解放	jiě fàng	Noun: liberation Verb: to liberate, to emancipate
昌盛	chāng shèng	Adjective: prosperous
对联	duì lián	Noun: rhyming couplet
过滤	guò lǜ	Noun: filtration Verb: to filter
精华	jīng huá	Noun: elite, essence
迷信	mí xìn	Noun: superstition
确立	què lì	Verb: to establish
体谅	tǐ liàng	Verb: to empathize, to show understanding
战斗	zhàn dòu	Noun: fight, battle Verb: to fight, to battle
侃侃而谈	kǎn kǎn ér tán	Verb: to speak in a calm and frank manner
偿还	cháng huán	Verb: to reimburse, to repay
队伍	duì wu	Noun: troops, ranks
过失	guò shī	Noun: error, fault, mistake
精简	jīng jiǎn	Verb: to simplify
密度	mì dù	Noun: density
确切	què qiè	Adjective: exact, definite
体面	tǐ miàn	Noun: dignity, face Adjective: honourable
兴致勃勃	xìng zhì bó bó	Verb: to be in high spirits
占据	zhàn jù	Verb: to occupy, to hold
砍伐	kǎn fá	Verb: to hew
兑现	duì xiàn	Verb: to cash (cheque, etc.)

过问	guò wèn	Verb: to ask about, to concern with
兢兢业业	jīng jīng yè yè	Adjective: cautious and conscientious
密封	mì fēng	Verb: to seal up, to seal airtight
确信	què xìn	Verb: to be sure, to be certain of
体系	tǐ xì	Noun: system, setup
凶恶	xiōng è	Adjective: fierce, evil, wicked
占领	zhàn lǐng	Verb: to capture, to occupy
克制	kè zhì	Noun: restrain, self-control Verb: to restrain
罪犯	zuì fàn	Noun: criminal
尝试	cháng shì	Noun: try, attempt Verb: to try, to attempt
对应	duì yìng	Verb: to correspond Adjective: corresponding, homologous
过瘾	guò yǐn	Verb: to satisfy a craving, to enjoy fully
精密	jīng mì	Noun: accuracy Adjective: exact, precise
免得	miǎn de	Conjunction: in order to avoid
群众	qún zhòng	Noun: the masses (people)
天才	tiān cái	Noun: talent, gift Adjective: talented, gifted
胸怀	xiōng huái	Noun: heart, mind, breadth of vision
战略	zhàn lüè	Noun: strategy
枯萎	kū wěi	Verb: to wither, to wilt
对照	duì zhào	Noun: comparison Verb: to compare, to contrast
过于	guò yú	Adverb: excessively, too much
惊奇	jīng qí	Verb: to be amazed, to be surprised
勉励	miǎn lì	Verb: to encourage
染	rǎn	Verb: to dye
天伦之乐	tiān lún zhī lè	Noun: family happiness
凶手	xiōng shǒu	Noun: murderer, assassin
战术	zhàn shù	Noun: tactics

哭泣	kū qì	Verb: to weep
场合	chǎng hé	Noun: situation, occasion
顿时	dùn shí	Adverb: at once, immediately, suddenly
嗨	hāi	Expression: Hi!
精确	jīng què	Adjective: accurate, precise
勉强	miǎn qiǎng	Verb: to do with difficulty, to force sbd. to do sth.
让步	ràng bù	Noun: concession Verb: to concede, to give in
天然气	tiān rán qì	Noun: natural gas
胸膛	xiōng táng	Noun: chest, thorax
战役	zhàn yì	Noun: battle, military campaign
苦涩	kǔ sè	Adjective: agonized, bitter
光荣	guāng róng	Noun: honour, glory Adjective: glorious, honourable
敞开	chǎng kāi	Verb: to open wide
哆嗦	duō suo	Verb: to tremble, to shiver, to quiver
海拔	hǎi bá	Noun: height above sea level
免疫	miǎn yì	Noun: immunity Adjective: immune
饶恕	ráo shù	Verb: to forgive, to spare
天生	tiān shēng	Adjective: innate, natural
雄厚	xióng hòu	Adjective: rich, abundant, solid
宽容	kuān róng	Adjective: tolerant, charitable
场面	chǎng miàn	Noun: scene, occasion
多元化	duō yuán huà	Noun: diversification, pluralism
海滨	hǎi bīn	Noun: shore, seaside
精通	jīng tōng	Verb: to be proficient
面貌	miàn mào	Noun: face, appearance
扰乱	rǎo luàn	Verb: to disturb
天堂	tiān táng	Noun: paradise, heaven

羞耻	xiū chǐ	Adjective: ashamed
章程	zhāng chéng	Noun: statute, rule
狼吞虎咽	láng tūn hǔ yàn	Verb: to eat hastily
场所	chǎng suǒ	Noun: location, place
堕落	duò luò	Verb: to degenerate, to corrupt
含糊	hán hu	Adjective: ambiguous, vague
经纬	jīng wěi	Noun: warp and woof, main points, longitude and latitude
面子	miàn zi	Noun: face, prestige
惹祸	rě huò	Verb: to stir up trouble
天文	tiān wén	Noun: astronomy
修复	xiū fù	Noun: restoration Verb: to repair, to restore
冷落	lěng luò	Verb: to cold shoulder sbd. Adjective: unfrequented, deserted
倡导	chàng dǎo	Verb: to initiate, to advocate
额外	é wài	Adjective: extra, additional
寒暄	hán xuān	Verb: to exchange conventional greetings, to make small talk
精心	jīng xīn	Adjective: meticulous, fine, detailed
描绘	miáo huì	Verb: to describe, to portray
热泪盈眶	rè lèi yíng kuàng	Verb: having one's eyes brimming with tears
田径	tián jìng	Noun: track and field, athletics
修建	xiū jiàn	Verb: to build, to construct
障碍	zhàng ài	Noun: barrier, obstacle, obstruction
礼尚往来	lǐ shàng wǎng lái	Expression: politely return received politeness
畅通	chàng tōng	Adjective: unblocked, free-flowing
恶心	ě xin	Noun: nausea Verb: to feel sick
含义	hán yì	Noun: meaning, implication
惊讶	jīng yà	Noun: astonishment, awe Adjective: surprised, amazed, astonished
渺小	miǎo xiǎo	Adjective: tiny, insignificant

热门	rè mén	Adjective: popular, in vogue
舔	tiǎn	Verb: to lick
帐篷	zhàng peng	Noun: tent
冒犯	mào fàn	Verb: to offend
畅销	chàng xiāo	Verb: to sell well
恶化	è huà	Verb: to worsen
罕见	hǎn jiàn	Adjective: rare, peculiar
精益求精	jīng yì qiú jīng	Verb: to keep improving sth. already outstanding
蔑视	miè shì	Noun: contempt Verb: to loath, to despise
仁慈	rén cí	Noun: benevolence, charity Adjective: benevolent, charitable
挑剔	tiāo ti	Adjective: picky, fussy
修养	xiū yǎng	Noun: training, self-cultivation, good manners
朝气蓬勃	zhāo qì péng bó	Verb: to be full of youthful energy
瞄准	miáo zhǔn	Verb: to target
倡议	chàng yì	Noun: proposal, initiative Verb: to suggest, to initiate
遏制	è zhì	Verb: to keep within limits, not letting the impact be too big
捍卫	hàn wèi	Verb: to defend, to uphold
精致	jīng zhì	Adjective: delicate, fine, exquisite
灭亡	miè wáng	Verb: to be destroyed, to become extinct, to perish
人道	rén dào	Noun: humanity, human sympathy
调和	tiáo hé	Noun: reconciliation Verb: to harmonize, to mediate
绣	xiù	Verb: to embroider
招收	zhāo shōu	Verb: to hire, to recruit
藐视	miǎo shì	Verb: to despise
恩怨	ēn yuàn	Noun: feeling of gratitude or resentment (at the same time)
航空	háng kōng	Noun: aviation

井	jǐng	Noun: well
民间	mín jiān	Adjective: popular, among the people
人格	rén gé	Noun: personality, integrity
调剂	tiáo jì	Verb: to adjust, to regulate, to fill a prescription
嗅觉	xiù jué	Noun: sense of smell
明智	míng zhì	Adjective: wise, sensible
钞票	chāo piào	Noun: paper money, bill
而已	ér yǐ	Expression: that's all, nothing more
行列	háng liè	Noun: line, row, procession
警告	jǐng gào	Verb: to warn, to admonish
人工	rén gōng	Adjective: artificial, man-made
调节	tiáo jié	Verb: to adjust, to regulate, to reconcile
虚假	xū jiǎ	Adjective: false, sham, dishonest
着迷	zháo mí	Verb: to be fascinated, to be captivated
南辕北辙	nán yuán běi zhé	Expression: to work in contradiction to the original plan
超越	chāo yuè	Verb: to surpass, to exceed
航天	háng tiān	Noun: space flight
警惕	jǐng tì	Verb: to be on the alert, to watch out for
人家	rén jia	Noun: household, family Pronoun: others, people, him/her, I
调解	tiáo jiě	Verb: to mediate, to conciliate
需求	xū qiú	Noun: requirement, demand
沼泽	zhǎo zé	Noun: swamp, marsh, wetlands
逆行	nì xíng	Verb: to go the wrong way (driving)
潮流	cháo liú	Noun: tide, current, trend
二氧化碳	èr yǎng huà tàn	Noun: carbon dioxide, CO2
航行	háng xíng	Verb: to sail, to fly, to navigate
颈椎	jǐng zhuī	Noun: cervical vertebra
敏捷	mǐn jié	Adjective: quick, nimble, agile

人间	rén jiān	Noun: this world
条款	tiáo kuǎn	Noun: clause, article, term
虚荣	xū róng	Noun: vanity
失事	shī shì	Verb: to have an accident (vehicle, plane, etc.)
偶像	ǒu xiàng	Noun: idol
朝代	cháo dài	Noun: dynasty
寺庙	sì miào	Noun: temple, monastery
发布	fā bù	Verb: to release, to issue
豪迈	háo mài	Adjective: bold, heroic
境界	jìng jiè	Noun: boundary, realm
敏锐	mǐn ruì	Adjective: keen, sharp, acute
人士	rén shì	Noun: person, public figure
条理	tiáo lǐ	Noun: orderliness, method, system
虚伪	xū wěi	Adjective: hypocritical
照样	zhào yàng	Adverb: in the same way as usual, as before
排练	pái liàn	Noun: rehearsal Verb: to rehearse
嘲笑	cháo xiào	Verb: to make fun of, to mock
发财	fā cái	Verb: to get rich
毫米	háo mǐ	Noun: millimetre
敬礼	jìng lǐ	Noun: salute
名次	míng cì	Noun: place in a competition, position in a ranking of names
人为	rén wéi	Adjective: artificial
调料	tiáo liào	Noun: flavouring, seasoning
须知	xū zhī	Noun: notice, information
照耀	zhào yào	Verb: shine, illuminate
片断	piàn duàn	Noun: fragment, segment
撤退	chè tuì	Verb: to withdraw, to retreat
发呆	fā dāi	Verb: to be lost in thought, to look absent-minded

毫无	háo wú	Adverb: not in the least, none whatsoever
竞赛	jìng sài	Noun: contest, competition
名额	míng é	Noun: quota of people
人性	rén xìng	Noun: human nature, humanity
条约	tiáo yuē	Noun: treaty, pact
许可	xǔ kě	Noun: permission Verb: to allow, to permit
平庸	píng yōng	Adjective: mediocre
撤销	chè xiāo	Verb: to repeal, to revoke
发动	fā dòng	Verb: to start, to launch, to arouse
耗费	hào fèi	Verb: to use, to waste
镜头	jìng tóu	Noun: camera lens, shot, movie scene
名副其实	míng fù qí shí	Verb: to be worthy of the name
人质	rén zhì	Noun: hostage
挑拨	tiǎo bō	Verb: to instigate, to stir up trouble, to provoke
酗酒	xù jiǔ	Noun: excessive drinking, alcohol abuse
遮挡	zhē dǎng	Verb: to shelter from
屏幕	píng mù	Noun: screen
沉淀	chén diàn	Noun: sediment, deposit Verb: to settle, to precipitate
竞选	jìng xuǎn	Verb: to run for office, to take part in election
明明	míng míng	Adverb: obviously, undoubtedly
忍耐	rěn nài	Verb: to exercise patience, to restrain oneself
挑衅	tiǎo xìn	Noun: provocation Verb: to provoke
畜牧	xù mù	Noun: animal husbandry
折腾	zhē teng	Verb: to do sth. over and over again, to toss about (sleepless)
启蒙	qǐ méng	Verb: to enlighten, to instruct
宇宙	yǔ zhòu	Noun: universe, cosmos
陈旧	chén jiù	Adjective: old, old-fashioned, antiquated

发觉	fā jué	Verb: to become aware, to find, to discover
号召	hào zhào	Verb: to call, to appeal
纠纷	jiū fēn	Noun: dispute, entanglement
名誉	míng yù	Noun: reputation, honour, fame
忍受	rěn shòu	Verb: to bear, to endure
跳跃	tiào yuè	Verb: to jump, to hop, to skip
序言	xù yán	Noun: preface, prologue
折	zhé	Verb: to break, to bend, to fold, to discount
气质	qì zhì	Noun: personality, temperament
陈列	chén liè	Verb: to display, to exhibit
发射	fā shè	Verb: to start, to fire, to launch
呵	hē	Expression: oh, ah
纠正	jiū zhèng	Verb: to correct, to put right
命名	mìng míng	Verb: to give a name to
认定	rèn dìng	Verb: to believe firmly
停泊	tíng bó	Verb: to anchor, to berth at
宣誓	xuān shì	Verb: to swear an oath, to make a vow
折磨	zhé mó	Noun: torment Verb: to torment
窍门	qiào mén	Noun: trick, recipe for success
挨	ái	Verb: to endure, to suffer
沉闷	chén mèn	Adjective: oppressive, depressing, dull
发誓	fā shì	Verb: to vow, to swear
和蔼	hé ǎi	Adjective: kind, amiable
酒精	jiǔ jīng	Noun: alcohol, ethanol
摸索	mō suǒ	Verb: to fumble, to feel about
认可	rèn kě	Noun: approval, acknowledgement Verb: to approve, to accept
停顿	tíng dùn	Noun: pause, halt Verb: to pause, to come to a standstill

宣扬	xuān yáng	Verb: to publicize, to propagate, to make well known
珍贵	zhēn guì	Adjective: precious, valuable
儒家	rú jiā	Noun: Confucianism
癌症	ái zhèng	Noun: cancer
陈述	chén shù	Verb: to state, to declare, to make a statement
发行	fā xíng	Verb: to publish, to issue, to distribute, to release
合并	hé bìng	Verb: to merge, to unite, to incorporate
救济	jiù jì	Verb: to give relief to, to succour
膜	mó	Noun: membrane, film
任命	rèn mìng	Verb: to appoint, to nominate
停滞	tíng zhì	Verb: to stagnate
悬挂	xuán guà	Verb: to hang, to suspend
侦探	zhēn tàn	Noun: detective
亲密	qīn mì	Adjective: intimate
骚扰	sāo rǎo	Verb: to harass
爱不释手	ài bù shì shǒu	Verb: not wanting to give sth. out of one's hand, to fondle admiringly
沉思	chén sī	Verb: to ponder, to muse, to mediate, to contemplate
发炎	fā yán	Noun: inflammation Verb: to inflame Adjective: inflamed
合成	hé chéng	Noun: compound, synthesis Verb: to compose, to constitute, to synthesize Adjective: synthetic
就近	jiù jìn	Location: nearby
摩擦	mó cā	Noun: friction, rubbing Verb: to rub against
任性	rèn xìng	Adjective: wilful, headstrong, capricious
亭子	tíng zi	Noun: pavilion
旋律	xuán lǜ	Noun: rhythm, melody
珍稀	zhēn xī	Adjective: rare and precious

尚且	shàng qiě	Conjunction: even (not)
乘	chéng	Verb: to ride on, to multiply
缘故	yuán gù	Noun: reason, cause
爱戴	ài dài	Verb: to love and respect
沉重	chén zhòng	Adjective: heavy, serious
发扬	fā yáng	Verb: to develop, to enhance
就业	jiù yè	Verb: to take up a job
模范	mó fàn	Noun: model, fine example
任意	rèn yì	Adverb: arbitrary, at will, at random
挺拔	tǐng bá	Adjective: tall and straight
悬念	xuán niàn	Noun: suspense (movie, play, etc.), concern
真相	zhēn xiàng	Noun: actual facts, truth
生肖	shēng xiào	Noun: animal from Chinese zodiac
暧昧	ài mèi	Adjective: ambiguous, equivocal, dubious
沉着	chén zhuó	Adjective: composed, cool headed, calm
发育	fā yù	Noun: development, growth Verb: to develop
合伙	hé huǒ	Verb: to cooperate, to form a partnership
就职	jiù zhí	Verb: to assume office, to take office
魔鬼	mó guǐ	Noun: devil
任重道远	rèn zhòng dào yuǎn	Verb: the burden is heavy and the road is long
通货膨胀	tōng huò péng zhàng	Noun: inflation
悬崖峭壁	xuán yá qiào bì	Noun: cliffside
真挚	zhēn zhì	Noun: sincerity Adjective: sincere, cordial
视频	shì pín	Noun: video, short video
称心如意	chèn xīn rú yì	Verb: to have everything one could wish for
法人	fǎ rén	Noun: legal person
和解	hé jiě	Noun: reconciliation, compromise Verb: to settle (a dispute out of court), to reconcile

鞠躬	jū gōng	Verb: to bow
磨合	mó hé	Verb: to get familiar with
仍旧	réng jiù	Adverb: still, yet
通俗	tōng sú	Adjective: popular, understandable
旋转	xuán zhuǎn	Verb: to rotate, to spin
珍珠	zhēn zhū	Noun: pearl
首饰	shǒu shì	Noun: jewellery
安宁	ān níng	Noun: peace Adjective: peaceful, tranquil
称号	chēng hào	Noun: title, term of address
番	fān	Verb: to take turns Measure Word: times
和睦	hé mù	Noun: peaceful relations, harmony Adjective: harmonious
拘留	jū liú	Noun: detention Verb: to detain, to arrest
模式	mó shì	Noun: mode, pattern
日新月异	rì xīn yuè yì	Verb: to change with each passing day
通用	tōng yòng	Adjective: commonly used, interchangeable
选拔	xuǎn bá	Verb: to choose, to select
斟酌	zhēn zhuó	Verb: to consider, to deliberate, to weigh
疏远	shū yuǎn	Noun: estrangement Verb: to drift apart
安详	ān xiáng	Adjective: composed, serene
橙	chéng	Noun: orange (fruit) Adjective: orange (colour)
繁华	fán huá	Adjective: flourishing
和气	hé qi	Adjective: friendly, amiable
拘束	jū shù	Adjective: reticent, constrained, awkward
魔术	mó shù	Noun: magic
日益	rì yì	Adverb: more and more each day, increasingly
同胞	tóng bāo	Noun: brother or sister by blood, fellow citizen, compatriot

选手	xuǎn shǒu	Noun: athlete, player
阵地	zhèn dì	Noun: front, position
瞬间	shùn jiān	Noun: moment
安置	ān zhì	Verb: to find a place for, to arrange for
盛	chéng	Verb: to hold, to fill
繁忙	fán máng	Adjective: busy
居住	jū zhù	Verb: to reside, to live
模型	mó xíng	Noun: model, mould, matrix, pattern
溶解	róng jiě	Noun: solution, dissolution Verb: to dissolve, to melt
童话	tóng huà	Noun: fairy tale
削弱	xuē ruò	Verb: to weaken
镇定	zhèn dìng	Adjective: cool, calm
素食	sù shí	Noun: vegetarian food
案件	àn jiàn	Noun: legal case, case
承办	chéng bàn	Verb: to undertake, to accept a contract
繁体字	fán tǐ zì	Noun: traditional character
合算	hé suàn	Verb: to reckon up Adjective: worthwhile, be worth the money
局部	jú bù	Adverb: in part, partial, local
抹杀	mǒ shā	Verb: to erase, to deny, to write off
容貌	róng mào	Noun: appearance, looks
振奋	zhèn fèn	Verb: to inspire, to stimulate
索取	suǒ qǔ	Verb: to demand, to request
案例	àn lì	Noun: case (law)
承包	chéng bāo	Verb: to contract, to undertake
繁殖	fán zhí	Verb: to breed, to reproduce
和谐	hé xié	Adjective: harmonious
局面	jú miàn	Noun: situation, aspect
莫名其妙	mò míng qí miào	Verb: unable to make head or tail of it

容纳	róng nà	Verb: to contain, to have the capacity of, to hold
同志	tóng zhì	Noun: comrade Adjective: homosexual
学说	xué shuō	Noun: theory, doctrine
震惊	zhèn jīng	Verb: to shock, to astonish
陶醉	táo zuì	Noun: euphoria Verb: to be enchanted by
按摩	àn mó	Noun: massage Verb: to massage
城堡	chéng bǎo	Noun: castle
反驳	fǎn bó	Verb: to retort, to refute
嘿	hēi	Expression: hey
局势	jú shì	Noun: situation
默默	mò mò	Adverb: silently, quietly
容器	róng qì	Noun: container, vessel
统筹兼顾	tǒng chóu jiān gù	Verb: to make a plan taking into account all factors
学位	xué wèi	Noun: academic degree
镇静	zhèn jìng	Adjective: calm, cool, composed
讨好	tǎo hǎo	Verb: to curry favour with sbd.
暗示	àn shì	Noun: hint, suggestion Verb: to hint, to suggest
成本	chéng běn	Noun: costs (production, etc.)
反常	fǎn cháng	Adjective: unusual, abnormal
痕迹	hén jì	Noun: mark, trace, vestige
局限	jú xiàn	Noun: limit Verb: to limit, to confine
墨水儿	mò shuǐ r	Noun: ink
融洽	róng qià	Adjective: harmonious
统计	tǒng jì	Noun: statistics
雪上加霜	xuě shàng jiā shuāng	Verb: to add frost to snow
阵容	zhèn róng	Noun: line-up (sports), troop arrangement

体裁	tǐ cái	Noun: genre, form of writing
昂贵	áng guì	Adjective: expensive, costly
惩罚	chéng fá	Noun: punishment Verb: to punish
狠心	hěn xīn	Adjective: heartless, cruel-hearted
举动	jǔ dòng	Noun: action, activity, movement
谋求	móu qiú	Verb: to seek, to strive for
容忍	róng rěn	Verb: to tolerate, to put up with
统统	tǒng tǒng	Adverb: completely, entirely
血压	xuè yā	Noun: blood pressure
振兴	zhèn xīng	Verb: to develop, to promote, to vitalize
天赋	tiān fù	Noun: talent, gift
凹凸	āo tū	Adjective: bumpy, uneven
成交	chéng jiāo	Verb: to reach a deal, to complete a contract
恨不得	hèn bu de	Verb: to have an itch to do sth., wish one could do sth.
咀嚼	jǔ jué	Verb: to chew
模样	mú yàng	Noun: look, style, appearance
揉	róu	Verb: to knead, to massage, to rub
投机	tóu jī	Verb: to speculate Adjective: opportunistic, congenial
熏陶	xūn táo	Verb: to nurture, to influence positively
通缉	tōng jī	Verb: to list as wanted (a criminal)
熬	áo	Verb: to endure, to suffer, to boil for a long time
承诺	chéng nuò	Noun: promise, commitment Verb: to promise, to agree to
反感	fǎn gǎn	Noun: resentment, antipathy, disfavour
哼	hēng	Expression: to express dissatisfaction
沮丧	jǔ sàng	Adjective: dispirited, dejected, depressed
母语	mǔ yǔ	Noun: native language
柔和	róu hé	Adjective: soft, mild, gentle

投票	tóu piào	Noun: poll Verb: to vote
循环	xún huán	Noun: circle, loop Verb: to cycle, to circulate
争端	zhēng duān	Noun: controversial issue, point in dispute
投诉	tóu sù	Noun: complaint Verb: to complain, to file a complaint
消灭	xiāo miè	Noun: annihilation Verb: to eliminate, to perish
奥秘	ào mì	Noun: mystery, secret
澄清	chéng qīng	Verb: to clarify Adjective: clear, limpid
反抗	fǎn kàng	Verb: to resist, to rebel
哄	hōng	Expression: roar of laughter
目睹	mù dǔ	Verb: to witness, to see with own eyes
弱点	ruò diǎn	Noun: weakness, weak point
投降	tóu xiáng	Noun: surrender Verb: to surrender
巡逻	xún luó	Verb: to patrol
争夺	zhēng duó	Verb: to fight for, to contend for
透露	tòu lù	Verb: to reveal
塔	tǎ	Noun: tower
扒	bā	Verb: to hold on to, to climb, to strip off
成天	chéng tiān	Adverb: all day long
反馈	fǎn kuì	Noun: feedback
烘	hōng	Verb: to bake, to warm by a fire
举世瞩目	jǔ shì zhǔ mù	Verb: to attract worldwide attention
目光	mù guāng	Noun: sight, view, vision
若干	ruò gān	Pronoun: some, a few Number: a certain number
投掷	tóu zhì	Verb: to throw, to toss
寻觅	xún mì	Verb: to look for
蒸发	zhēng fā	Noun: evaporation Verb: to evaporate

吞吞吐吐	tūn tūn tǔ tǔ	Expression: to beat around the bush
疤	bā	Noun: scar
反面	fǎn miàn	Noun: the other side, reverse side
轰动	hōng dòng	Verb: to cause a great sensation, to make a stir
举足轻重	jǔ zú qīng zhòng	Verb: to play the decisive role
沐浴	mù yù	Verb: to take a bath
撒谎	sā huǎng	Verb: to tell lies
秃	tū	Adjective: bald, blunt
循序渐进	xún xù jiàn jìn	Adverb: step by step
征服	zhēng fú	Verb: to conquer, to subdue
唾弃	tuò qì	Verb: to disdain
巴不得	bā bu de	Verb: to be eager to, to look forward to
呈现	chéng xiàn	Verb: to appear, to show, to present
反射	fǎn shè	Noun: reflection Verb: to reflect
剧本	jù běn	Noun: screenplay
拿手	ná shǒu	Verb: to be good at
突破	tū pò	Verb: to break through, to make a breakthrough
争气	zhēng qì	Verb: to try to make a good showing, be determined not to fall short
蔚蓝	wèi lán	Adjective: azure, sky blue
巴结	bā jie	Verb: to flatter, to fawn
成效	chéng xiào	Noun: effect, result
反思	fǎn sī	Verb: to rethink, to think over again
宏观	hóng guān	Adjective: macroscopic
聚精会神	jù jīng huì shén	Verb: to concentrate completely
纳闷儿	nà mèn r	Verb: to feel puzzled, to wonder
图案	tú àn	Noun: design, pattern
压迫	yā pò	Verb: to oppress, to repress
征收	zhēng shōu	Verb: to levy, to impose, to collect

无辜	wú gū	Noun: innocence Adjective: innocent
拔苗助长	bá miáo zhù zhǎng	Verb: to spoil things through a wish for quick results
成心	chéng xīn	Adverb: on purpose, deliberately
反问	fǎn wèn	Noun: rhetorical question, counter question
洪水	hóng shuǐ	Noun: flood, deluge
剧烈	jù liè	Adjective: acute, violent, severe
耐用	nài yòng	Adjective: durable
散文	sǎn wén	Noun: prose, essay
徒弟	tú dì	Noun: apprentice
压岁钱	yā suì qián	Noun: money given to children during Spring Festival
争先恐后	zhēng xiān kǒng hòu	Verb: to strive to be the first and fear to be the last
物业	wù yè	Noun: property, real estate
把关	bǎ guān	Verb: to check on, to guard a pass
成员	chéng yuán	Noun: member
反之	fǎn zhī	Conjunction: on the other hand, conversely
宏伟	hóng wěi	Adjective: grand, imposing, magnificent
据悉	jù xī	Verb: it is reported
难得	nán dé	Adjective: rare
散发	sàn fā	Noun: emission, distribution Verb: to emit, to distribute
途径	tú jìng	Noun: way, approach, route
压缩	yā suō	Noun: compression Verb: to compress, to squeeze, to reduce
争议	zhēng yì	Noun: dispute, controversy
陷阱	xiàn jǐng	Noun: trap, pitfall
把手	bǎ shou	Noun: handle, knob
诚挚	chéng zhì	Adjective: sincere, cordial, earnest
范畴	fàn chóu	Noun: category
喉咙	hóu lóng	Noun: throat, larynx

决策	jué cè	Noun: (strategic) decision Verb: to make policy, to make a strategic decision
难堪	nán kān	Adjective: embarrassed, embarrassing, humiliating
丧失	sàng shī	Verb: to lose, to forfeit
涂抹	tú mǒ	Verb: to paint, to smear
压抑	yā yì	Verb: to constrain, to oppress Adjective: oppressive, stifling, depressing
正月	zhēng yuè	Noun: first month of the lunar year
主义	zhǔ yì	Expression: ...ism
潇洒	xiāo sǎ	Adjective: handsome, chic, confident
嚷	rǎng	Verb: to blurt out, to shout
秤	chèng	Noun: steelyard
泛滥	fàn làn	Verb: to flood, to overflow, to spread unchecked
吼	hǒu	Verb: to roar, to howl, to shout
绝望	jué wàng	Noun: desperation, hopelessness Verb: to despair, to lose courage
嫂子	sǎo zi	Noun: wife of older brother
土壤	tǔ rǎng	Noun: soil, earth
压榨	yā zhà	Verb: to press, to squeeze, to extract juice by squeezing
挣扎	zhēng zhá	Verb: to struggle, to agonize over
玉	yù	Noun: jade
花瓣	huā bàn	Noun: petal
心甘情愿	xīn gān qíng yuàn	Verb: to be delighted to do sth.
霸道	bà dào	Verb: to rule by might Adjective: overbearing, dictatorial, arbitrary
吃苦	chī kǔ	Verb: to bear hardships, to suffer
贩卖	fàn mài	Verb: to sell, to peddle
后代	hòu dài	Noun: later generations, descendants, offsprings
觉悟	jué wù	Noun: consciousness, awareness Verb: to become aware of

难能可贵	nán néng kě guì	Adjective: commendable, estimable
团结	tuán jié	Noun: rally Verb: to unite, to join forces, to hold a rally
压制	yā zhì	Verb: to suppress, to inhibit, to stifle
整顿	zhěng dùn	Verb: to consolidate, to reorganize, to tidy up
喧哗	xuān huá	Noun: hubbub, roar, noise
罢工	bà gōng	Noun: strike Verb: to go on strike
吃力	chī lì	Adjective: strenuous, requiring effort
方位	fāng wèi	Noun: direction, position
后顾之忧	hòu gù zhī yōu	Noun: worries about future consequences
觉醒	jué xǐng	Verb: to awake, to come to realize
恼火	nǎo huǒ	Verb: to get angry, to be annoyed
刹车	shā chē	Noun: brake Verb: to brake (car)
团体	tuán tǐ	Noun: group, organization, team
亚军	yà jūn	Noun: runner-up, second place
正当	zhèng dāng	Adjective: honest, fair, sensible Conjunction: just when
悬殊	xuán shū	Noun: difference, disparity
掰	bāi	Verb: to break with both hands
迟缓	chí huǎn	Adjective: slow, sluggish, tardy
方言	fāng yán	Noun: dialect
军队	jūn duì	Noun: army
内涵	nèi hán	Noun: intention, meaning
啥	shá	Pronoun: what
烟花爆竹	yān huā bào zhú	Noun: fireworks and crackers
正负	zhèng fù	Adjective: positive and negative
炫耀	xuàn yào	Verb: to show off
持久	chí jiǔ	Adjective: lasting, persistent, enduring
方针	fāng zhēn	Noun: policy, guidelines

后勤	hòu qín	Noun: logistics
卡通	kǎ tōng	Noun: cartoon
内幕	nèi mù	Noun: inside story Location: behind the scenes
筛选	shāi xuǎn	Noun: screening Verb: to sieve out, to filter
推测	tuī cè	Noun: speculation Verb: to speculate, to guess, to presume
淹没	yān mò	Verb: to submerge, to drown, to flood out
正规	zhèng guī	Adjective: regular, according to standards
截止	jié zhǐ	Noun: deadline Noun: to put a stop to, to close
鸦雀无声	yā què wú shēng	Expression: absolute silence
摆脱	bǎi tuō	Verb: to get rid of, to break out of, to free oneself from
防守	fáng shǒu	Verb: to defend, to protect
候选	hòu xuǎn	Noun: candidate
开采	kāi cǎi	Verb: to exploit, to mine
内在	nèi zài	Adjective: inherent, intrinsic
山脉	shān mài	Noun: mountain range
推翻	tuī fān	Verb: to overthrow, to overturn, to reverse, to topple
沿海	yán hǎi	Location: coastal, along the coast
正经	zhèng jing	Adjective: decent, honourable
岳母	yuè mǔ	Noun: wife's mother
拜访	bài fǎng	Verb: to pay a visit, to call on
迟疑	chí yí	Verb: to hesitate
忽略	hū lüè	Verb: to neglect, to overlook
开除	kāi chú	Verb: to dismiss, to expel
能量	néng liàng	Noun: energy, capacity, ability
闪烁	shǎn shuò	Verb: to twinkle, to glimmer, to flicker
推理	tuī lǐ	Noun: reasoning, inference
严寒	yán hán	Adjective: freezing, very cold

正气	zhèng qì	Noun:	healthy atmosphere, righteousness
招标	zhāo biāo	Verb:	to tender, to invite bids
败坏	bài huài	Verb:	to ruin, to corrupt, to undermine
赤道	chì dào	Noun:	equator
防御	fáng yù	Noun: defence Verb: to defend, to guard	
呼啸	hū xiào	Verb:	to whistle, to scream, to howl
开阔	kāi kuò	Verb: to widen, to open up Adjective: wide, open	
擅长	shàn cháng	Verb:	to be good at
推论	tuī lùn	Noun: deduction, reasoned conclusion Verb: to infer	
严禁	yán jìn	Verb:	to strictly prohibit
政权	zhèng quán	Noun:	regime, political power
震撼	zhèn hàn	Verb:	to stun, to shock
协调	xié tiáo	Verb:	to coordinate, to harmonize
拜年	bài nián	Verb:	to wish a Happy New Year
赤字	chì zì	Noun:	deficit (financial)
防止	fáng zhǐ	Verb:	to prevent, to avoid
呼吁	hū yù	Noun: appeal Verb: to appeal	
开朗	kāi lǎng	Adjective:	optimistic, easy-going
拟定	nǐ dìng	Verb:	to draw up, to formulate
擅自	shàn zì	Adverb: without permission, on one's own initiative	
推销	tuī xiāo	Verb:	to market, to sell
严峻	yán jùn	Adjective:	serious, grim, severe
证实	zhèng shí	Verb:	to confirm, to verify
正宗	zhèng zōng	Adjective:	traditional, authentic, old school
拜托	bài tuō	Expression: Please!	
充当	chōng dāng	Verb:	to serve as, to act as
防治	fáng zhì	Noun:	prevention and cure

胡乱	hú luàn	Adverb: carelessly, casually, at random
开明	kāi míng	Adjective: enlightened, open-minded
年度	nián dù	Noun: year
商标	shāng biāo	Noun: trademark, logo
严厉	yán lì	Adjective: strict, severe
证书	zhèng shū	Noun: credentials, certificate
之际	zhī jì	Conjunction: on the occasion of
谜语	mí yǔ	Noun: riddle
颁布	bān bù	Verb: to issue, to promulgate
冲动	chōng dòng	Noun: impulse
纺织	fǎng zhī	Verb: spinning and weaving
湖泊	hú pō	Noun: lake
开辟	kāi pì	Verb: to open up, to start
捏	niē	Verb: to pinch, to knead
伤脑筋	shāng nǎo jīn	Adjective: troublesome, knotty
脱离	tuō lí	Verb: to break away from, to separate oneself from
言论	yán lùn	Noun: speech, expression of opinion
正义	zhèng yì	Noun: justice Adjective: just, righteous
执着	zhí zhuó	Adjective: dedicated, stubborn
颁发	bān fā	Verb: to award, to issue
冲击	chōng jī	Noun: shock, strike, attack, impact
放大	fàng dà	Verb: to enlarge, to magnify
拧	níng	Verb: to twist, to wring, to pinch
上级	shàng jí	Noun: higher authorities, superiors
拖延	tuō yán	Noun: adjournment, procrastination Verb: to adjourn, to delay
严密	yán mì	Adjective: strict, tight, rigorous
郑重	zhèng zhòng	Adjective: serious, solemn
致力	zhì lì	Verb: to devote one's efforts to

凡是	fán shì	Adverb: every, any, all
充沛	chōng pèi	Adjective: abundant, plentiful
放射	fàng shè	Noun: radiation, emission Verb: to radiate, to emit
华丽	huá lì	Noun: gorgeous, magnificent
开拓	kāi tuò	Verb: to open up, to break new ground, to exploit
凝固	níng gù	Verb: to solidify, to congeal
托运	tuō yùn	Verb: to consign (goods), to check (baggage)
延期	yán qī	Verb: to delay, to postpone, to defer
症状	zhèng zhuàng	Noun: symptom
从容	cóng róng	Adjective: calm, unhurried
坠	zhuì	Verb: to drop, to fall
版本	bǎn běn	Noun: version, release
充实	chōng shí	Verb: to enrich, to replenish Adjective: substantial, rich
华侨	huá qiáo	Noun: overseas Chinese
开展	kāi zhǎn	Verb: to develop, to launch, to carry out
凝聚	níng jù	Verb: to condense, to coagulate
上任	shàng rèn	Verb: to take office
妥当	tuǒ dang	Adjective: appropriate, proper, suitable
炎热	yán rè	Adjective: burning hot, blistering hot
枝	zhī	Noun: branch Measure Word: for sticks, rods, pencils, etc.
滋润	zī rùn	Adjective: moist, humid
棉花	mián hua	Noun: cotton
伴侣	bàn lǚ	Noun: partner, mate
冲突	chōng tū	Noun: conflict, clash Verb: to conflict, to clash
非法	fēi fǎ	Adjective: illegal
化肥	huà féi	Noun: chemical fertilizer
开支	kāi zhī	Noun: expenses, expenditures

凝视	níng shì	Verb: to gaze, to stare
上瘾	shàng yǐn	Noun: addiction Verb: to be addicted to, to get into a habit
妥善	tuǒ shàn	Adjective: appropriate, proper, careful
延伸	yán shēn	Verb: to extend, to stretch, to spread
支撑	zhī chēng	Verb: to support, to prop up
伴随	bàn suí	Verb: to accompany, to follow
充足	chōng zú	Adjective: adequate, sufficient, abundant
飞禽走兽	fēi qín zǒu shòu	Noun: birds and animal
划分	huà fēn	Verb: to divide up, to mark off
刊登	kān dēng	Verb: to publish (in a newspaper, magazine, etc.)
宁肯	nìng kěn	Conjunction: would rather, would prefer
上游	shàng yóu	Location: upper reaches, advanced position
妥协	tuǒ xié	Noun: compromise Verb: to compromise, to reach terms
岩石	yán shí	Noun: rock
支出	zhī chū	Noun: expense Verb: to spend, to expend
半途而废	bàn tú ér fèi	Verb: to give up halfway
崇拜	chóng bài	Noun: adoration Verb: to adore, to worship
飞翔	fēi xiáng	Verb: to fly
画蛇添足	huà shé tiān zú	Verb: to overdo it, to ruin the effect by adding sth. superfluous
勘探	kān tàn	Noun: exploration Verb: to prospect for
宁愿	nìng yuàn	Conjunction: would rather, prefer to
梢	shāo	Noun: tip of a branch
椭圆	tuǒ yuán	Noun: ellipse Adjective: oval, elliptic
延续	yán xù	Verb: to continue, to last
脂肪	zhī fáng	Noun: fat (body)
扮演	bàn yǎn	Verb: to play the role of, to act

重叠	chóng dié	Noun: overlap, redundancy Verb: to overlap
飞跃	fēi yuè	Verb: to leap, to jump
化石	huà shí	Noun: fossil
刊物	kān wù	Noun: publication
纽扣儿	niǔ kòu r	Noun: button
捎	shāo	Verb: to pass on, to bring sth. to sbd.
演变	yǎn biàn	Verb: to evolve, to develop
知觉	zhī jué	Noun: perception, consciousness
绑架	bǎng jià	Noun: kidnapping Verb: to kidnap
崇高	chóng gāo	Adjective: lofty, sublime
肥沃	féi wò	Adjective: fertile
话筒	huà tǒng	Noun: microphone
看待	kàn dài	Verb: to look upon, to regard
扭转	niǔ zhuǎn	Verb: to reverse, to turn round
哨	shào	Noun: whistle, sentry
挖掘	wā jué	Verb: to dig, to excavate
掩盖	yǎn gài	Verb: to conceal, to cover up, to hide
支流	zhī liú	Noun: minor aspects, tributary (river)
榜样	bǎng yàng	Noun: example, model
崇敬	chóng jìng	Noun: respect Verb: to revere, to respect
诽谤	fěi bàng	Verb: to slander, to libel, to defame
化验	huà yàn	Noun: laboratory test, chemical analysis
浓厚	nóng hòu	Adjective: dense, thick, strong (interest), deep
奢侈	shē chǐ	Adjective: luxurious, extravagant
娃娃	wá wa	Noun: baby, small child, doll
眼光	yǎn guāng	Noun: vision, foresight
支配	zhī pèi	Verb: to control, to dominate
磅	bàng	Measure Word: for pound

化妆	huà zhuāng	Noun: make-up Verb: to put make-up on
慷慨	kāng kǎi	Adjective: generous, liberal, fervent
农历	nóng lì	Noun: traditional Chinese calendar, lunar calendar
涉及	shè jí	Verb: involve, concern
瓦解	wǎ jiě	Verb: collapse, disintegrate
掩护	yǎn hù	Noun: protection, cover Verb: to screen, to shield, to cover
支援	zhī yuán	Verb: to support, to provide assistance
民主	mín zhǔ	Noun: democracy Adjective: democratic
包庇	bāo bì	Verb: to shield, to cover up
废除	fèi chú	Verb: to abolish, to cancel, to abrogate
考察	kǎo chá	Verb: to inspect, to investigate
奴隶	nú lì	Noun: slave
设立	shè lì	Verb: to set up, to establish
哇	wa	Particle: oh
支柱	zhī zhù	Noun: pillar, backbone, mainstay
除	chú	Verb: to divide, to exclude Relative Clause: except for
包袱	bāo fu	Noun: burden, load
筹备	chóu bèi	Noun: preparation Verb: to get ready for, to prepare
沸腾	fèi téng	Verb: to boil, to reach ebullition
欢乐	huān lè	Noun: gladness, pleasure Adjective: happy, joyous, gay
考古	kǎo gǔ	Noun: archaeology
挪	nuó	Verb: to move, to shift
社区	shè qū	Noun: community
歪曲	wāi qū	Verb: to distort, to misrepresent
眼色	yǎn sè	Noun: wink, meaningful glance
知足常乐	zhī zú cháng lè	Verb: to be happy with what one has

特意	tè yì	Adverb: specially, expressly
包围	bāo wéi	Verb: to surround, to encircle
废墟	fèi xū	Noun: ruins
环节	huán jié	Noun: link, segment, connection
考核	kǎo hé	Verb: to examine, to assess, to evaluate
虐待	nüè dài	Noun: mistreatment Verb: to mistreat, to abuse
外表	wài biǎo	Noun: appearance
眼神	yǎn shén	Noun: expression in eyes, eyesight
值班	zhí bān	Verb: to be on duty, to work a shift
横	héng	Adjective: horizontal, across
包装	bāo zhuāng	Noun: package Verb: to pack
稠密	chóu mì	Adjective: thick, dense, intimate
分辨	fēn biàn	Verb: to distinguish, to defend oneself against an accusation
还原	huán yuán	Noun: reduction (chem.) Verb: to restore to the original state
考验	kǎo yàn	Noun: test, trial Verb: to test, to try
哦	ò	Expression: oh
摄氏度	shè shì dù	Noun: degree centigrade
外行	wài háng	Noun: amateur, laity Adjective: unprofessional
掩饰	yǎn shì	Verb: to conceal, to cover up
直播	zhí bō	Noun: live broadcast
保管	bǎo guǎn	Verb: to keep, to take care of
丑恶	chǒu è	Adjective: ugly, repulsive
分寸	fēn cun	Noun: judgement for propriety, propriety
缓和	huǎn hé	Verb: to ease, to relax, to moderate
靠拢	kào lǒng	Verb: to draw close, to close up
殴打	ōu dǎ	Verb: to beat up, to hit
设想	shè xiǎng	Verb: to imagine, to assume

外界	wài jiè	Noun: the outside world
演习	yǎn xí	Noun: exercise, practice, manoeuvre
殖民地	zhí mín dì	Noun: colony
饱和	bǎo hé	Noun: saturation Adjective: saturated
初步	chū bù	Adjective: initial, preliminary
吩咐	fēn fù	Verb: to instruct, to tell, to command
患者	huàn zhě	Noun: patient
磕	kē	Verb: to knock
设置	shè zhì	Verb: to install, to set up
外向	wài xiàng	Adjective: extrovert
职能	zhí néng	Noun: function, role
饱经沧桑	bǎo jīng cāng sāng	Verb: having lived through a lot of painful changes
出路	chū lù	Noun: way out (of difficulty)
分红	fēn hóng	Noun: bonus, dividend Verb: to draw dividend
荒凉	huāng liáng	Adjective: desolate
呕吐	ǒu tù	Verb: to vomit, to throw up
深奥	shēn ào	Adjective: deep, abstruse, profound
丸	wán	Measure Word: for pills, small balls, etc.
演绎	yǎn yì	Verb: to deduce, to infer
职位	zhí wèi	Noun: position, post, office
保密	bǎo mì	Verb: to keep sth. confidential, to maintain secrecy
出卖	chū mài	Verb: to sell, to sell out, to betray
分解	fēn jiě	Verb: to resolve, to break down, to decompose
科目	kē mù	Noun: subject, course
趴	pā	Verb: to lie on the stomach
申报	shēn bào	Noun: declaration Verb: to declare, to report, to register
完备	wán bèi	Adjective: complete, perfect, faultless

演奏	yǎn zòu	Verb: to perform music, to play (music)
职务	zhí wù	Noun: post, job, duties
撇	piē	Noun: stroke from top to left bottom
保姆	bǎo mǔ	Noun: nanny, housekeeper
出身	chū shēn	Noun: family background, origin
分裂	fēn liè	Noun: fission Verb: to split, to divide
荒谬	huāng miù	Adjective: absurd, ridiculous
可观	kě guān	Adjective: considerable, impressive, respectable
排斥	pái chì	Verb: to reject, to exclude, to repel
深沉	shēn chén	Adjective: deep, dull, heavy
完毕	wán bì	Verb: to complete, to finish
验收	yàn shōu	Verb: to verify and accept, to check on receipt
指标	zhǐ biāo	Noun: norm, index, target
保守	bǎo shǒu	Verb: to guard, to keep Adjective: conservative
出神	chū shén	Verb: to be lost in thought
分泌	fēn mì	Verb: to secrete
荒唐	huāng táng	Adjective: ludicrous, absurd, beyond belief, fantastic
可口	kě kǒu	Adjective: tasty, delicious
排除	pái chú	Verb: to eliminate, to remove, to get rid of
深情厚谊	shēn qíng hòu yì	Noun: profound friendship
顽固	wán gù	Adjective: stubborn, obstinate
厌恶	yàn wù	Verb: to hate, to detest, to loath
指定	zhǐ dìng	Verb: to appoint, to designate, to assign
庄稼	zhuāng jia	Noun: grain, crop
保卫	bǎo wèi	Verb: to defend, to safeguard
出息	chū xi	Noun: promise, prospects
分明	fēn míng	Adjective: clearly demarcated, distinct

黄昏	huáng hūn	Noun: dusk, nightfall
渴望	kě wàng	Verb: to thirst for, to long for
排放	pái fàng	Noun: emission Verb: to discharge, to void
绅士	shēn shì	Noun: gentleman
玩弄	wán nòng	Verb: to play with, to flirt
验证	yàn zhèng	Verb: to test and verify
指甲	zhǐ jia	Noun: fingernail
访问	fǎng wèn	Noun: visit Verb: to visit, to interview
融化	róng huà	Verb: to melt, to thaw
保养	bǎo yǎng	Noun: maintenance Verb: to maintain, to take care of one's health
分歧	fēn qí	Verb: differences, discrepancy
恍然大悟	huǎng rán dà wù	Verb: to suddenly realize
可恶	kě wù	Adjective: hateful, repulsive
徘徊	pái huái	Verb: to move around, to fluctuate, to hesitate
呻吟	shēn yín	Verb: to moan, to groan
顽强	wán qiáng	Adjective: tenacious, indomitable
氧气	yǎng qì	Noun: oxygen
指令	zhǐ lìng	Noun: order, instruction
卷	juǎn	Noun: roll Verb: to roll Measure Word: for roll, spool
荣幸	róng xìng	Adjective: honoured
保障	bǎo zhàng	Verb: to ensure, to guarantee
储备	chǔ bèi	Noun: reserves Verb: to store up
分散	fēn sàn	Verb: to disperse, to scatter
辉煌	huī huáng	Adjective: splendid, brilliant, glorious
派别	pài bié	Noun: faction, group, school of thought
神奇	shén qí	Adjective: miraculous, mystical

玩意儿	wán yì r	Noun:	toy
样品	yàng pǐn	Noun:	sample, specimen
指南针	zhǐ nán zhēn	Noun:	compass

Congratulations! You have successfully finished studying all HSK vocabularies!

If you found this vocabulary guide helpful, please do us a favour and post a comment wherever you have purchased this book to let other learners know about your experiences.

Thank you & Good luck with the test!

Printed in Great Britain
by Amazon